THE Cultural Dimensions OF Educational Computing

Understanding the Non-Neutrality of Technology

C. A. BOWERS

Teachers College, Columbia University
New York and London

Published by Teachers College Press, 1234 Amsterdam Avenue,
New York, NY 10027

Library of Congress Cataloging-in-Publication Data

Bowers, C. A.
The cultural dimensions of educational computing.

(Advances in contemporary educational thought ; 1)
Bibliography: p.
Includes index.
1. Education—Data processing. 2. Computer-assisted instruction. 3. Educational technology.
4. Educational anthropology. I. Title. II. Series.
LB1028.43.B68 1988 371.3′9445 88-12365

ISBN 0-8077-2923-X

Manufactured in the United States of America

93 92 91 90 89 88 1 2 3 4 5 6

Contents

Foreword

In order to advance thought, we must sometimes step back to achieve a broader perspective on what we are doing without thinking deeply about it. Building on his earlier work, which utilized a sociology of knowledge and historical-cultural perspective, Bowers here offers a conceptual framework for developing his thesis that technology is not, as is commonly believed, a neutral tool of society or the educator.

In this work, Bowers focuses on the ubiquitous computer and its growing use in instruction. He asks us to reflect on the computer as it mirrors our twentieth-century technocratic mind-set. He argues that its use reinforces and strengthens our historical-cultural view of knowledge as power, as the harbinger of progress, and our view of the individual as autonomous and self-directed. He claims that it is this same mind-set that has created a world of serious ecological imbalance and cataclysmic nuclear threat, as well as a breakdown of symbolic processes and a loss of our sense of community. He urges us to think of the computer as a mediator of culture as we increasingly move to the full use of computers in education.

Whatever else education is, it certainly is one of society's key vehicles for the transmission of culture. The school transmits more than information. It also passes on, often in subtle and indirect ways, the metaphors that translate our history and traditions into meaningful symbols. The computer, however, is taken to be primarily a neutral and highly efficient machine for the storage and retrieval of information. Bowers argues that it cannot be neutral. In the design of programs, even the most free and flexible interactive type, the mind of the programmer is reflected in the form the subject matter takes and the processing possibilities provided. There is always a bias in the program, and not necessarily an individual bias; most often it is a cultural one. A gender bias, a racial bias, a technological bias, for example, can be passed on in the guise of neutral presentation. The instructional computer is a vehicle of cultural transmission.

Bowers wants to restore to our discussions and thinking about educational computing a serious consideration of the role and responsibility of the teacher as mediator of the student's understanding of culture. In his view, teachers should not be merely the skilled users of computer-assisted instruction; they must be reflective practitioners who question the mind-set of the programmer and the cultural forces at work in the learning environment created by the computer in the classroom. He also warns Third World educators who are eager to use the latest technology to achieve modernization that there are dangers of Western cultural bias built into the seemingly neutral devices of computer-assisted instruction.

In this contribution to the Teachers College Press Advances in Contemporary Educational Thought series, Bowers forces us to reflect on computing and education from a broad and deep historical-cultural perspective. Readers may not accept his formulations of the issues or his solutions to problems, but I do not see how any reader can ever again view the computer as a technical rather than as a cultural device. This is truly to advance our thinking and take us to a realm where the most fundamental questions about our responsibilities as educators must be asked.

Jonas F. Soltis, Editor
Advances in Contemporary
Educational Thought Series

Acknowledgments

One of the main themes of this book is that while thought is, in part, a unique process carried out by an individual, most of what is thought about—including the conceptual categories used to organize ideas, values, relationships, and so forth—is rooted deeply in the symbolic processes and patterns of the cultural group. This applies to the field of computer science and to the specialists who are attempting to develop the educational uses of this new technology; it also applies to my own arguments. Much of my analysis focuses on how educational computing incorporates a number of unexamined traditions of thought that reproduce in the present the misconceptions of the past—about the nature of technology, language, individualism, and the rational process, as well as about how knowledge is represented. But what is not made explicit in the analysis are the traditions of thought that have provided the vocabulary and ways of thinking that made it possible for me to reframe the educational and cultural issues associated with educational computing. These traditions need to be recognized, in part, as a way of acknowledging my indebtedness to individual thinkers who demonstrated the ability to challenge, extend, and, in some instances, redirect the conceptual traditions of their time. A second reason is to remind the reader that while my interpretations and extensions of arguments may be legitimately challenged, the conceptual frameworks used to formulate these arguments cannot simply be dismissed as Bowers's idiosyncratic point of view. The foundations of my analysis are grounded in the sociology of knowledge of Alfred Schutz, the hermeneutic and linguistic traditions of Martin Heidegger, Friedrich Nietzsche, and Gregory Bateson, and the cultural perspectives of Mary Douglas, Clifford Geertz, and Walter Ong. I am also indebted to feminist thinkers, most notably Sandra Harding and Susan Bordo, who are addressing the epistemological foundations of gender dominance, and to a myriad of thinkers who are helping to clarify the extent to which the thought process is metaphorical—including Mark Johnson, Michael Reddy, and George Lakoff. Lastly, the awareness that these traditions of thought relate directly to understanding the deeper cultural dynamics of educational computing was originally prompted by books authored by Hubert and Stuart Dreyfus, Theodore Roszak, Joseph Weizenbaum, and Douglas Sloan. If my analysis could be reduced to a single point, it would be that educational computing is more properly and fully understood within the conceptual frameworks of these thinkers than the traditions of thought that go back to René Descartes, Frederick Taylor, and B. F. Skinner—which seem to be the current, and largely unacknowledged, conceptual foundations of the field.

The actual process of writing was facilitated by a number of graduate students—some in educational computing and some in educational studies: Susan Harrington, Mohammad Atar, Billy C. Yates, and Douglas Cooper. Their criticisms of early drafts were invaluable. Extended conversations with Ron Scollon and Deborah Tannen helped to crystalize my understanding of certain aspects of language and its relationship to technology. Pattie Nelson, educational computer assistant for the Eugene School District, provided access to needed instructional software. And the typing of the many drafts was performed by Phyllis Wells, to whom I owe a special thanks.

Lastly, it is difficult to acknowledge adequately the part played by my wife, Mary Bowers, in supporting and guiding the development of the manuscript. She provided the initial encouragement to write the book, the ongoing support needed during those times when the writing seemed to drag, and the critical perspective on ideas that were in their formative stage.

The Cultural Dimensions of Educational Computing

Understanding the Non-Neutrality of Technology

CHAPTER 1

The Cultural Context of Educational Computing

The groundswell of enthusiasm surrounding the use of computers in the classroom seems to be at a critical point. It is difficult to tell whether it is a temporary disturbance, like the rock that momentarily disturbs the placid surface of the water, or a building force that will sweep across and transform the most basic educational patterns. If it is a temporary phenomenon, even now in a receding state, it is possible that by the time this book appears computers will have been relegated to the marginal status of an educational tool—thus repeating the cycle that characterized television. A more likely development, given the tremendous versatility of computer technology, is that it will be a transforming force but one that retains its place as an educational tool rather than as a technology that dictates the patterns of learning and social interaction.

Not being able to judge accurately the ascent of a movement, it is necessary to keep in mind that any analysis of the educational implications of computers must be general. A criticism directed at keyboards may be made irrelevant, for example, by further developments in the use of voice commands. But there is another reason for undertaking a more general discussion of computers in the classroom, and that has to do with the fact that a number of educational issues transcend specific technologies, such as a computer, which are introduced into the classroom. In a sense these transcendent issues relate more to judging the educational consequences of the technologies (e.g., textbooks, television, microcomputers), but such issues are not addressed by the experts who design the technologies for making learning more efficient and predictable. By identifying these issues and placing them within the larger conceptual framework necessary for thinking about the educational and social consequences of the new technologies, I will also clarify both my relationship to the subject under discussion and my special areas of competency.

I am not a hacker who delights in the intellectual challenge of writing programs, nor do I find the second level of involvement (learning to match the power of the program with the more instrumental purposes of the software) to be especially interesting. My intellectual preference for books over computers, however, does not mean that I am anticomputer or that I do not find computers interesting as an educational and cultural phenomenon. Quite the contrary. My interests (and area of expertise) relate more to the conceptual, ideological, and cultural side of the technology. The manner in which computers influence patterns of communication and the structure of knowledge, mediate the individual's sensory relationship with the environment, and re-encode the vocabularies of the culture, while at the same time influencing what gets saved and what gets lost in the transmission process, leads to extremely important questions that should be considered by educators.

The view that a computer expert requires a knowledge of programming or the procedures that unlock the calculating and information-processing power of the machine reflects our cultural practice of segmenting experience into discrete components and of thinking that expertise is acquired by learning about and technologically mastering that component part. The problem with this form of thinking is that it fails to recognize that the discrete entities we isolate for study are an integral part of a complex ecology that includes both the cultural and natural environment. This cultural pattern of thinking works, in a sense, like lenses that enable us to see certain entities while putting other aspects out of focus. When we think that expertise in the area of computers involves only a technical form of knowledge for using and improving computers, we are, in fact, under the influence of the conceptual guidance system of our culture. In terms of the cultural bias built into our way of thinking, new ideas and technologies are understood as progressive by their very nature. But what is not as clearly recognized is that the new forms of knowledge and technologies often lead to unanticipated consequences whose disruptions may outweigh any gains from the innovations. The use of computers in the classroom is simply the most recent experiment with the fabric of culture. A knowledge of the educational uses of computers (to be computer literate, to use the jargon) should also involve an understanding of how this new technology alters the cultural ecology of the classroom as well as influences the larger culture.

The tunnel vision that results from our cultural tendency to abstract one element from the ecology of relationships is particularly problematic when it is used in the area of education. Textbooks and teacher guides on how to use microcomputers in the classroom serve as the best evidence of this tunnel vision. In addition to developing the special vocabulary that permits entry into the guild, there is a near-total emphasis on the technical aspects of application. What is not discussed are the questions of how the use of microcomputers might relate to the broader purposes of education, including a consideration of the forms of educational empowerment needed at this point in our cultural development. The people who are adapting microcomputers for classroom use appear to think of the educational relationship in terms of four component parts: the software program, students as users of the new technology, information to be processed, and the teacher (who occupies a more ambivalent role). That the dynamics of the classroom are historically shaped by cultural forces and that the students will subsequently spend their adult lives making political decisions that either contribute to the amelioration of our cultural deficiencies or help to perpetuate them appear to be largely irrelevant issues to the people who promote the educational uses of microcomputers. For them, the main purpose of education is to learn how to use data as the basis of thinking.

Understanding how the educational use of computers influences our pattern of thinking, and thus contributes to changes in the symbolic underpinnings of the culture, should be considered an essential aspect of computer literacy. In order to encourage viewing the educational use of computers in this broader perspective, I want to elaborate on Joseph Weizenbaum's observation that "the problems facing schools and educators everywhere are personal, political, financial, and spiritual. These will not be solved merely by putting more terminals and video screens into the classroom" (quoted in Long, 1985, p. 49).

As the creator of ELIZA (an early natural language program) and a professor at MIT, Weizenbaum represents the inside perspective that sees more clearly the limitations of the new technology. If computers themselves cannot be used to provide an educational, political, and moral sense of direction for schools, as his comment suggests, then it is necessary to take seriously the argument that the sense of direction for education must, in part, be based on a careful consideration of the problems we face as a society and the ameliorative role that schools should play.

Seriously discussing the connection between education and culture, particularly what needs to be preserved and what needs reforming, is infinitely more difficult than deciding which software program should be used. This is because the discussion must, of necessity, move into the political realm, where it is difficult to reach consensus on even the most basic level of identifying which cultural traditions are worth preserving and which should be reformed. Teachers, like other members of society, often assume the authoritativeness of their own perspectives on these matters. The result is that the political process of identifying the most pressing social issues, which will help to decide the broader purposes of education, often degenerates to the level where agreement is limited to "agreeing to disagree." Faced with futility of the moral and political relativism that usually overwhelms any attempt at clarifying our social priorities for reform, most teachers find making decisions about the use of technology in the classroom a more manageable process. I should like to go against the grain of this tendency by laying out the argument that the sense of direction for public schools must take account of those aspects of our culture that are problematic for all social groups. This is not a matter of reaching agreement on the design of a new culture; but it does involve identifying the most serious problems we face and a general sense of the direction in which we must move if the problems are to be ameliorated. This will provide us with a tentative conceptual compass for assessing how the use of computers in the classroom relate to the ongoing problem of cultural renewal.

After we have established the larger conceptual framework for thinking about schools, the discussion in subsequent chapters will focus on the educational issues that arise when computers are used in the classroom. These chapters will be used to challenge the widely held myth that computers are a neutral technology, as well as to identify what teachers must understand about the influence of computers on the cultural transmission process if they are to develop a more clinical understanding of its educative effects. The term *clinical* is used here to suggest that if teachers understand the dynamic interplay among culture, language, and the thought process—and how the classroom use of computers fits into this symbolic environment—they will be able to recognize more clearly the different decisions that must be made in directing the educational process and what the educative effects of their decisions will be. This clinical awareness, which applies as well to the use of other technologies in the classroom (e.g., books, films, television), is essential to restoring the importance of the teacher's judgment in the educational process. But first we must examine how the classroom reinforces a particular social orientation—and thus cannot be viewed separately from the larger questions pertaining to the cultural traditions that need to be preserved and those that need radical reform.

That the classroom reinforces a particular set of social patterns and beliefs seems a truism that does not need to be stated. Yet the textbooks and journal articles explaining how to use computers in the classroom are nearly uniform in maintaining the myth that the technical questions of a computer-based educational program have no social implications beyond that of providing students with a high level of skill mastery. As Martin Siegel and Dennis Davis (1986) noted in the last chapter of a very long book on computer-based education: "We cannot say precisely what the impact of a high level of instructional effectiveness will be on the culture" (p. 229).

But as their two-page discussion of the "Impact on Schools and Society" suggests, the effects could only be considered as positive. Siegel and Davis, like many other advocates of using computers in education, assume that more efficient mastery of skills automatically contributes to social progress; but they ignore the question of what kind of future we are progressing toward.

The classroom is not only a microcosm of the larger society; it also contributes to the future direction the society will take. Patterns of thinking, status systems, social norms, and an economic-political orientation are transmitted to the students as part of the language environment of the classroom. These information codes are taught concomitantly with the explicit curriculum and thus generally escape the attention of teachers, who often transmit them as part of the unexamined beliefs they share with students. This fund of tacit knowledge becomes an essential aspect of the students' conceptual (and political) guidance system that enables them to fit into the patterns that regulate adult life. These information codes are taught as teachers enforce the cultural norms that include, among others, allocating the rights of turn-taking in social interaction, the relationships between conceptual categories as well as the appropriate content of each, the way in which competitive individualism is to be legitimately expressed, the basis of authority for moral and intellectual decisions, and how to use time efficiently.

As the language systems (verbal and nonverbal, print, spatial) used in the classroom reinforce the cultural patterns sustained through everyday conversation in the larger society, it is difficult to separate the classroom from the achievements and deficiencies of society. The connection between classroom and society is further complicated by the fact that not all the cultural patterns and orientations are treated equally in the classroom. To put it another way, the classroom strengthens certain cultural orientations by communicating them to the young and weakens others by not communicating them. The cultural orientations that are strengthened generally relate to the technological consumer domain of society: attitudes toward technological innovation, the progressive nature of change, measurement and planning as sources of authority, a conceptual hierarchy that places abstract-theoretical thought at the highest, a competitive-remissive form of individualism, and the definition of human needs in terms of what can be supplied by a commodity culture. The cultural orientations that are weakened in the classroom include the forms of authority and skills associated with the oral traditions: folk arts and technologies, substantive traditions of the community (excluding, of course, high school athletics), the fine arts, and the values related to what Wendell Berry (1970) referred to as care, competence, and frugality in the use of the world.

An important question is whether the current state of computer technology used in the classroom strengthens those cultural orientations contributing to a technicist social order and weakens others that cannot be integrated into the new emerging order. A second possibility is that the computer is a neutral technology and that its influence on the direction of cultural change merely reflects the biases of the software producer and classroom teacher. This is the position that most computer advocates take, but it is not based, as we shall see, on a careful consideration of evidence. A preliminary analysis of present educational software (which retains many of the qualities of the print technology found in textbooks) reveals the view of rationality that underlies modern technology, particularly with its emphasis on facts (objective knowledge) that can be rationally manipulated in order to provide the authority for decision making. The current technology also strengthens the view of individualism as autonomous and self-directing and reinforces the belief that change can be rationally planned (Winograd and Flores, 1986). Aside from important questions relating to whether the educational uses of computers benefit certain social groups unequally, the deeper concerns relate to what has become a cultural manifest destiny that cuts across class and ethnic distinctions. These concerns, which pertain more generally to Weizenbaum's warning about taking seriously our sense of moral, political, and spiritual direction as a people, must be taken into account when assessing the consequences of integrating the new technology into the educational process.

In spite of the excessively heavy burden of responsibilities that most teachers face, it is necessary to identify the most critical dimensions of the crisis we face as a culture. This is essential if teachers are going to have a reference point for deciding whether their curricular decisions, including their use of computer software programs, contribute to the crisis or are part of the solution. These judgments, of course, are never as simple as our conceptual categories suggest; nevertheless, it is essential that teachers possess a general sense of how their activities relate to the more powerful forces at work in the culture. This also applies to the people who write the educational software. As stated earlier, their work extends beyond the packaging of facts and devising of new and more efficient information-management systems; the ultimate effect of their technical innovations is to influence the thought patterns of the student and, in the process, contribute to the conceptual foundations necessary for furthering particular orientations within the culture.

As we face, on one end of the continuum, the prospects of a massive miscalculation in the nuclear arms race and, on the other, a growing disparity of wealth between the First and Third Worlds, it may appear a bit ridiculous to suggest that there are three aspects of the crisis that are of particular concern to those making decisions about the education of youth. Either the near-term crisis (possibility of nuclear warfare) or the long-term crisis (the population explosion and resource depletion in the Third World) may overwhelm us, thus nullifying the ameliorative efforts of teachers and others who are striving to improve the prospects of the human condition. But it can be argued that those aspects of the current crisis that educators should use as a moral and conceptual reference point are indeed related to the crisis that now encompasses the entire world. Perhaps more important is the need to identify those aspects of the crisis that are so close to home that they actually intrude into the classroom and are affected by the values and ideas that are being taught. Although it can be debated whether the three aspects of the crisis that are identified in the following sections are the most important ones (some will argue that the class struggle is the only issue that deserves serious attention, while others will claim that gender oppression remains unresolved), the critical point in terms of considering the use of computers is to recognize that the facts, ideas, and values—as well as the tacit cultural patterns that serve to organize our explicit knowledge in ways we are not generally aware of—must be judged in terms of the cultural orientations they reinforce.

TECHNOLOGICAL MIND-SET AND THE ECOLOGICAL CRISIS

For the last 20 years evidence has been accumulating on a massive scale that supports Barry Commoner's warning that "the way in which we now live on the earth is driving its thin, life-supporting skin, and ourselves with it, to destruction" (1972, p. 17). A long list of books, beginning with Raymond Dasmann's *Environmental Conservation* (1959/1968) and Rachel Carson's *Silent Spring* (1962), have documented the misuse of the environment through the introduction into the ecosystem of more than 40,000 commercially produced chemicals, the destruction of top soil for the sake of short-term gains in agricultural productivity, and the rapid depletion of fossil fuels (with the concomitant release into the atmosphere of carbon dioxide)—as consumer expectations rise all the while. In addition to marshaling the evidence of growing environmental abuse, this literature has also identified certain elements of the Western belief system as the chief source of the problem. It is this belief system that needs to be more fully understood if we are to avoid reinforcing in the classroom the very mind-set that is contributing to this part of the crisis.

One of the great ironies of human history is that the mind-set that has produced an incredible rate of technological change (resulting in an increased material standard of living for many, as well as a prolonged life) is also responsible for pillaging the environment to the extent that its life-sustaining processes are being threatened. Many of the elements of this mind-set are responsible for genuine achievements in civil society (protection of civil liberties, greater equality of opportunity in education and workplace); but because of historical developments these same elements, when related to the technological-economic domain of society, have evolved into a way of thinking that is now characterized by the arrogance of the expert's knowledge that results from a misreading of its achievements. By interpreting rationality, progress, and efficiency in terms of technological achievements, this mind-set has developed the hubris that leads to viewing the ecological crisis as requiring a further technological fix rather than the recognition that our most fundamental patterns of thinking may be faulty.

It is possible to identify the characteristics of this increasingly dominant mind-set that tends to view all aspects of experience in terms of problems that require technical solutions. Although many of its roots are deeply embedded in the humanitarian vision of the Enlightenment, it has become in recent years narrowed, specialized, and calculating. In its present form this mind-set recognizes only explicit forms of knowledge that allow for an abstract-theoretical formulation of the problem. Explicit knowledge is thus interpreted as that which can be observed, treated as a fact or as a quantifiable, calculable measure. The implicit forms of knowledge that are part of every form of cultural activity (adjusting the unspoken rules that govern the use of different language systems—spoken, body, space, time, and so forth—to changes in social context, performing skills, and pursuing activities) are thus not taken into account (Douglas, 1975). In addition to discounting the implicit knowledge that enables us to be effective cultural beings, the technicist mind-set devalues the importance of context. The technicist reflects upon the situation as a theoretical exercise, establishes what constitutes the essential component parts (and their working relationships), and reconceptualizes the components into a more rational system that can be utilized in a variety of contexts. Experimentation with the actual operation of the new system (either a new social technique like the *Distar* reading program or a mechanical technique) is seen as producing measurable data that determine both efficiency and effectiveness. The overriding ideal of this mind-set is the creation of a model or program that is not context-specific but has universal application. The underlying methaphor involves viewing the world as a machine; thus the task of the rational-calculating mind is simply to re-engineer the various systems in order to improve prediction, control, and efficiency.

This mind-set assumes that each technical innovation, each problem solved, represents progress. Thus reason and progress are fused together, and the alternative sources of authority that might serve as a brake on this magnificent engine of progress are treated as reactionary and unenlightened forms of thinking. Traditional practices, beliefs, technologies, and architectural forms that have evolved over time may simply be replaced by a new technology that is disconnected from context, which includes implicit forms of knowledge that sustain both the everyday lives of people and a sense of historical continuity. In effect, the technicist mind-set privileges experimental innovation over substantive traditions, abstract and theoretical ways of thinking over implicit forms of understanding, the autonomous individual over the collective memory and interdependence of the cultural group, and a reductionist, materialistic view of reality that denigrates the forms of spiritual discipline necessary for living harmoniously with other forms of life that make up the Gaia of planet earth.

When tied to a form of economy that requires a continual growth in consumer expectation, where yesterday's luxuries become today's necessities, we can see how this mind-set puts us on a trajectory that leads to ecological breakdown. As E. F. Schumacher observed, "An attitude toward life which seeks fulfillment in the single-minded pursuit of wealth—in short, materialism—does not fit into this world, because it contains within itself no limiting principle, while the environment in which it is placed is strictly limited" (1973, p. 27).

This lack of a self-limiting principle has, in fact, been viewed as a virtue by the humanists who declared in "A Secular Humanist Declaration" that we must "look to the natural, biological, social, and behavioral sciences for knowledge of the universe and man's place within it" (1981, p. 59). To limit the discovery of knowledge (which must conform to the canons of rational empiricism), the development of new technologies, the self-expression of individuals within the marketplace, and the potential of our economy to create new markets would be as close to heresy as we can get in the secular world. Yet this is exactly what Schumacher and others concerned with adjusting the voracious energies of our culture are advocating. The bottom line is bringing our incessant drive to press outward on the frontiers of basic research, technological innovation, and a consumer-based standard of living into line with the requirements for long-term habitation of the planet. Thus the real challenge we face is to rethink the most basic aspects of our belief system and social practice in terms of the emerging politics of bioregionalism (Porritt, 1984; Sale, 1986; Snyder, 1980).

Public schools contribute to this strange and dangerous paradox where the forms of knowledge that are supposed to empower and uplift the level of consciousness contribute, at the same time, to the rapid deterioration of the ecosystems. The problem facing the schools is twofold. Schools have become the chief means of providing the conceptual foundations necessary for the advanced knowledge required to operate and develop further the sophisticated technologies upon which our consumer society now depends. This involves teaching students to think in a manner that is compatible with the social-engineering processes that keep our commodity culture from falling into a state of permanent destabilization. Students thus learn to think in abstract-decontextualized ways, segment experience into component parts, recognize that the quantification of experience represents the highest source of intellectual authority, consume courses as units of learning, acknowledge the hierarchical structure of knowledge that requires certified experts, and view time in personal terms of self-advancement (i.e., escape from the traditions of an outmoded past).

While this conceptual matrix is being reinforced through the packaging of school knowledge, the school also contributes to intensifying a second problem associated with a technicist-commodity culture. This is the problem that Ivan Illich has identified as the modernization of poverty. The fragmentation of experience into specializations requiring certified knowledge to use the increasingly sophisticated technologies has, at the same time, undermined the ability to use "personal endowment, communal life, and environmental resources" in an independent manner (Illich, 1977, p. xii). Tools that traditionally had use-value in terms of enabling people to sustain themselves and control the patterns of their lives are no longer available, partly because our form of schooling reinforces the cognitive patterns that make a virtue of abstract-decontextualized knowledge. Those who cannot acquire this form of knowledge, and the certificates that allow them to intervene as experts in a specialized area of problem solving, leave school with a diminished sense of self and largely ignorant of how to use the tools that have been used for centuries to provide the necessary basis of a meaningful social existence. As the forms of knowledge necessary for communal self-sufficiency have no legitimate standing in the school curriculum, students who cannot (or will not) learn to think in a manner that makes them dependent upon a consumer orientation leave school without necessary life-supporting and community-organizing skills. They become, as anomic individuals, wards of the welfare bureaucracy, viewed as a necessary casualty of social progress.

CRISIS OF LIBERAL IDEOLOGY: INDIVIDUALISM AND COMMUNITY

The continuity between the patterns of thought taught in the classroom and our emphasis on a technological approach to production and social problem solving can also be seen in how the crisis of liberal ideology penetrates into the classroom. The assumptions underlying the worldview of liberalism cannot be separated from the growing list of ecological problems or the increasing influence of the technicist mentality over the regulation of daily affairs. The argument can easily be made that liberalism, with its assumptions about change, human nature, and the efficacy of rational thought, provided an important part of the conceptual framework necessary for the development of a strong technological orientation. An argument can also be made that the power of this technological approach to problem solving has resulted in a greater ability to collect and store data, thus providing the information base for an expansion in the ability of the state to intervene and regulate the life of the individual. Understanding the conceptual relationships among liberalism, the rise of the state, and the spread of the technicist way of thinking into every aspect of social life is important to understanding another irony that often escapes the attention of those who accept ideals on their own terms and thus fail to examine the dark side of social practice. The irony relates to how the rise of the state and the spread of technicist thinking are dependent upon the liberal image of the individual as an autonomous, self-directing being (Bowers, 1986).

Many educators who have made this view of the individual the capstone of their educational practice and social vision fail to realize the metaphorical nature of language: most important, that individualism is a metaphor that has been associated with profoundly different images. At one time the image of the individual was associated with being a subject within a feudal social order, later it was connected with being a citizen, and today it means, in some quarters, being the absolute source of authority on all matters and thus a self-creating entity. In this more contemporary view, the individual, often described in terms of being free and equal, is supposed to exercise critical choice while being unencumbered by the constraints of community and tradition. But in discounting the importance of both memory and external forms of authority, the autonomous individual has few reference points for either exercising critical reflection or resisting the interventions of the state and the shaping forces of the technicist mode of thinking. The form of individualism that is grounded in the myth of autonomy and self-direction has, in effect, only the defense of subjective judgment—a form of relativism that is easily overwhelmed by the agents of social engineering, who can marshal massive amounts of data to justify the implementation of new technologies.

Although the liberal view of individualism has become in recent years tied directly to the growth of technicism (and accompanying ecological problems), our real concern here is with that part of the crisis in liberal thought that relates to the relationship of the individual to the community. Within educational circles the liberal ideal of the individual is expressed in terms of the notion that education will enable the individual to be more rational and thus more self-directing. The economic counterpart of this view is that the pursuit of self-interest will maintain the competitive environment necessary for social progress and for rewarding individual efforts. Politically, this view of individualism makes the process of government contingent upon the aggregate of consenting individuals. Although the liberal ideal of making the individual the basic social unit has been seriously undermined by the expansion of the power of the state to regulate everyday life, as well as changes in the world economic system, the ideal still exerts a profound influence on thought. This growing discrepancy between liberal ideology and social practice does not, however, lead to resolving the problem of how to reconcile the interests of the individual with those of the community.

Although there has been a recent revival of a sense of community (as islands of interdependency, mutual responsibility, and work directed toward the achievement of shared goals), the dominant economic and political trends continue to reinforce a more anomic and rootless form of social relationship. A community that empowers its individual members as well as itself represents a political unit that must have its own conceptual foundations of authority, and thus it does not fit easily into the social-engineering scheme of corporations who want to open up or close down plants—depending on their profitability. Nor do strong communities yield easily to the dictates of politicians and bureaucrats who, in viewing the world from a more abstract vantage point, impose policies that often ignore the local context. The possibility of viable communities may be further weakened by internal processes, including a form of education that strengthens a form of rootless individualism by socializing students to a decontextualizing form of thinking, by ignoring the forms of knowledge and values essential to the authority of community life, and by reinforcing the liberal ideology that represents the person as an autonomous, self-directing individual. In effect, the educational process carried on in schools may equip the individual to operate within the larger society by undermining the symbolic foundations of the community.

The problem of reconciling the liberal view of individualism, which is ultimately concerned with the problem of individual empowerment, with the needs of the community can be partly resolved by questioning the basis for viewing the individual as an autonomous being. Unlike John Locke, one of the originators of the contemporary view of self-interest individualism, we need to situate the individual within the community by asking whether the individual has a reciprocal and interdependent relationship or is, as Locke assumed, autonomous and essentially self-sufficient except for certain needs that only government can meet. To put it bluntly, are individuals an interdependent part of a complex symbolic message system and food chain or do they have an autonomous and self-sufficient existence?

By recognizing our interdependent relationship within the food chain and the culturally derived language that makes possible thought and communication, we are forced to broaden our understanding of community. Although the myth of self-interest has created an ambivalent attitude toward the authority of the social community, it has largely governed our relations with the biotic community. As a result we have tended to ignore, as Gary Snyder points out, that the air, soil, water, plants, and animals are part of an interdependent system that includes even those individuals who operate according to the egocentric myth that they are responsible to whatever is dictated by self-interest or rational thought (usually a more disguised form of self-interest). But Snyder's view of community membership goes beyond individuals who relate to each other for instrumental and bureaucratic purposes (to get things done, so to speak). Context, for Snyder, adds to the sense of self a spiritual as well as an ecological dimension: "We must find our way to seeing the mineral cycles, the water cycles, air cycles, nutrient cycles, as sacramental—and we must incorporate that insight into our own personal quest and integrate it with all the wisdom teachings we have received from the nearer past. The expression of it is simple: gratitude to it all, taking responsibility for your own action; keeping contact with the sources of energy that flow into your own life (i.e., dirt, water, flesh)" (1977, p. 63). Or as Kirkpatrick Sale put it, "We must try to understand ourselves as participants in and not masters over [the] biotic community" (1986, p. 24).

COMPUTERS AND THE PANOPTICON SOCIETY

The suggestion that educators give serious attention to the cultural orientation they are reinforcing in the classroom will sound to many readers like more academic rhetoric. They are likely to admit that the environment has been badly misused, and some may even be prepared to acknowledge the danger of carrying the ideal of the autonomous individual to an extreme. But admitting the existence of the problem does not necessarily make it real at the level of concrete experience, the level at which one has to act upon it. A more likely feeling, one that serves to insulate against these seemingly abstract warnings, is that the progress associated with past experience (especially when we rely upon science and technology) will continue into the future and that the problems of environment and community will somehow lose their importance; at the very least, they will eventually be displaced on TV by new social concerns that have greater audience holding power. Warnings about the consequences of depleting the ozone layer, of acid rain on our forests and lakes, of the extinction of up to 25 percent of the earth's species over the next two decades, and of raising the earth's temperature—all these seem remote when compared to the immediate social consequences of missing a mortgage payment or making a misstep in carrying out the social routines that underlie everyday experience. Nevertheless, one new development within our culture has attracted increasing attention at the immediate level of personal experience—the fact that computer technology has increased the power of people who have access to data, while leaving many others vulnerable to an increasing degree of technological surveillance.

A new time frame has been introduced by technology; where once time was meaningfully reckoned in units of hours, minutes, and seconds, it is now measured in nanoseconds (billionths of a second). In addition to speeding up the processing of data, the change makes possible the massive collection of data on more aspects of daily life. We are not yet of one mind about the social and political consequences of this new technology. Some people celebrate the use of a technology that promises to process data in a time frame beyond the threshold of what humans can experience; many others, however, are becoming aware of new constraints imposed by the surveillance (data-collecting) capacity of this new technology. In *Silicon Shock*, Geoff Simons compared the awesome capacity of computers with that of human communication:

> Imagine . . . two computers conversing with each other over a period. They are then asked by a human being what they are talking about, and in the time he takes to pose the question, the two computers have exchanged more words than the sum total of all words exchanged by human beings since *Homo sapiens* first appeared on earth 2 or 3 million years ago. (1985, p. 165)

Although this comparison must be understood as metaphorical, it suggests a technological capacity that needs to be understood from a perspective that is generally ignored; namely, the psychological, social, and political consequences that result from the process of collecting the massive amounts of data necessary to justify the development of even more powerful computers. Not all of computing relates to solving engineering problems. The use of computers to store and process data pertaining to all aspects of human experience is now an accepted aspect of modern life. Consumer choices, political behavior, educational experiences, and work place productivity—as well as the nature of nearly all interactions of a citizen with a public or private institution—are recorded in an increasingly interlocking network of data bases.

This capacity for surveillance at the micro level of human activity—the ability to collect and collate details on test scores, telephone calls, consumer purchases, foreign travel, reading habits, political involvement, and so forth—can be understood in a manner quite different from John Naisbitt's facile summary of this new cultural path we are evolving along. According to him, "The new power is not money in the hands of the few, but information in the hands of the many" (1982, p. 7). Michel Foucault, the French social philosopher, provides a more accurate and politically disturbing phrase for describing what computer technology now makes possible: the panopticon society.

The principle of panopticism goes back to the ideas of Jeremy Bentham, the British Utilitarian philosopher who conceived the idea of a circular prison where a centrally located tower would allow prison guards to keep all inmates under constant surveillance. The major effect of the panopticon, according to Foucault, is "to induce in the inmate a state of consciousness and permanent visibility that assures the automatic functioning of power" (1979, p. 201). Power, as Foucault explains it, is expressed through "a set of actions upon other actions" (1983, p. 220). The exercise of power that alters relationships and forms of activities can be expressed in many ways: the design of physical space, the spoken word, the gaze of the other, the data-based decision of the expert, the rule-following administrator, and so forth. What is important about Foucault's analysis of how power is exercised over the subject in the panopticon prison is his understanding that their awareness that they are objects of constant surveillance would cause the prisoners to police themselves. Thus the design of the prison becomes essential for the exercise of a particular form of power, making the prisoners feel the continual presence of a disciplinary practice. The technology for maintaining this surveillance thus integrates the prisoner, as an unconscious collaborator, into a network of power relationships that shape social practices and limit human possibilities. As Foucault observes, the prisoners themselves become the "bearers" of the panopticon society.

Foucault's understanding of how power is expressed in disciplinary and controlling practices is not limited to a single culture or set of social arrangements. His analysis of Bentham's panopticon technology can be extended into other areas of social life—education, work, leisure, health care, and so forth—and is particularly useful for recognizing how a technology that operates in the time frame of a nanosecond can contribute to bringing more areas of social life under the panopticon principle. To put it more directly, the flip side of the data processing coin is data collection, and the scale of data collection through electronic monitoring is what makes possible the political nightmare of the panopticon society.

While the increased capacity for surveillance is directly related to technological advances in computing, its promotion is dependent upon cultural values that extend much further back in our history. A vice president of a data processing firm used two of these values (efficiency and data) to justify the use of monitoring systems in the work place: "We are letting management make better, quicker decisions based on facts, not opinions" (Koepp, 1986, p. 46). As these values have come to be viewed more and more as basic to achieving progress, there has been a huge increase in the use of surveillance technology in the work place. In the areas of telecommunications and service contacts (e.g., telephone and insurance companies, airlines, banks, etc.), sophisticated software programs keep track of every aspect of the worker's performance. According to Gary Marx and Sanford Sherizen, two researchers interested in the use of surveillance technology, 20,000 systems were sold in the United States that have the capacity to record such information as what telephone is used to make a call, what user identification code and extension is used, where the call goes, what time it is made, and how long it lasts (Marx & Sherizen, 1986, p. 66).

Similar technology used by an airline company collects data on how long each of its 400 reservation clerks spend on each call and how much time elapses before they pick up their next one. Workers earn negative points if they repeatedly use more than 109 seconds in handling a call or take more than 12 minutes in bathroom trips. Truck drivers have their performance monitored by a small computer aptly named Tripmaster. Speed, gear shifts, amount of time the engine idles, and time used for coffee breaks are all recorded on a printout. Even the key strokes of the typist can be electronically recorded, so that compensation can be exactly calibrated to performance. In one data-processing firm, for example, an employee who performs five keystrokes a second (18,000 per hour) earns the top salary. Computer-based surveillance technology has become so sophisticated that data collected elsewhere on the worker's use of drugs off the job site can be retrieved by the employer, with the result that the traditional distinction between private and public life is now being blurred.

The workplace, however, is not the only arena of social life that reflects the growth of panopticism. In assessing the surveillance and data recording capacity of the federal government, Theodore Roszak notes that five major federal agencies now hold over two billion files on individual citizens; the networking of computer-based surveillance can be seen in the growth of data exchanges between federal agencies and businesses in the private sector. In addition to the practice of accessing private sector data bases as a way of monitoring the activities of private citizens, federal agencies now share data with credit-reporting companies whose files contain information on "life style," employment record, credit worthiness, delinquent alimony payments, and so forth. In reflecting on how the widespread use of surveillance technology is being allowed to change the political relationship between the citizen and the process of government without a vote of the people, Roszak writes that "what we confront in the burgeoning surveillance machinery of our society is not a value-neutral technological process; it is, rather, the social vision of the utilitarian philosophers (Bentham and his followers) at last fully realized in the computer. It yields a world without shadows, secrets, or mysteries, where everything has become a naked quantity" (Roszak, 1986, p. 187). In this increasingly panopticon society, individuals internalize the new technology of social control by adjusting their behaviors and thoughts in accordance with the categories and logic that will constitute a positive personal data profile, and in the process become, like the prisoners, self-monitoring.

Given educators' long-standing verbal commitment to nurturing the student's intellectual and moral growth, one might have expected them to resist the intrusion of panopticism into the classroom. But as Foucault noted, Bentham's principle of panoptic control was first adopted by teachers and auxiliary social workers who considered data to be essential for measuring the progress of students. This same penchant for developing more efficient teaching procedures, and for collecting data to determine the effectiveness of classroom procedures, has led to viewing the management of the instructional process as one of the major challenges in computer application. A school-instructional management program implemented in a Utah school district, called A.I.M. (Achieving Instructional Mastery), is a good example of how far the technology (and human will) has evolved in bringing all aspects of school life under the data-recording gaze of the computer.

The A.I.M. system, according to one critical observer, is designed to monitor student progress "toward teacher-defined objectives," as well as to record assignments, tests, and grades in an electronic gradebook; it also keeps data on school attendance and lunch period activities and provides for the analysis of all recorded data (Callister, 1986). As part of an integrated surveillance system, it has the capacity to record student behavior in accordance with an elaborate classification system and to correlate behavior with academic performance. The A.I.M. system is interesting for several reasons. First, the computerized management approach to instruction necessitates that the core curriculum be organized in terms of objectives that fit the objective evaluation format of the management program. This required that only true/false or multiple-choice responses be elicited from the students and that faculty teach to objectives that are specified in advance. The instructional management system not only provides teachers with precise data on student performance, but also brings the teacher's performance under more direct surveillance by the school district administrators. Second, by being in a classroom where there is continual monitoring of activities, students are learning that surveillance is essential to the development of the socially responsible citizen, and thus could be expected to view it as a normal, even necessary, aspect of adult life.

The use of the computer to collect data on all aspects of the school is not unique to the A.I.M. system used in the Utah school district. Although other school districts across the country may not have adopted such a totalizing monitoring system, nearly all have some parts of a data-processing system and, driven by a technicist way of thinking that equates data with sound decision-making, are moving further in the direction of turning the school into a model of the panopticon society.

The technological orientation of school administrators and of teachers who advocate the educational use of computers brings us back to the basic questions about the cultural orientations that are reinforced in the classroom and about the teacher's responsibility for helping students understand the underlying values and beliefs that foster our particular form of technological progress. The use of computers in the classroom reinforces a different conceptual orientation than does the use of books, which stimulate the imagination and force an engagement with complex figures that are genuine metaphors of human life. Whether the computer has certain inherent characteristics that reinforce a technicist mentality or is, like a pencil, neutral in that it can be used by a Martin Luther King, Jr., or an Adolf Hitler, is a question we will return to later. It will suffice for now to establish the importance of the question to any future consideration of the legitimate role of computers in the classroom and what students should be taught about the nature of this technology.

SITUATING MICROCOMPUTERS WITHIN THE ECOLOGY OF THE CLASSROOM: AN OVERVIEW

In the following chapters we shall be viewing the microcomputer as part of the cultural transmission that goes on in a classroom. The processes and issues that will be put in focus are relevant to understanding the educational consequences that follow the use of any technology—whether it is an alphabet, a pencil, or a microcomputer. But our main concern will be with understanding how the microcomputer fits into the cultural ecology of the classroom—and with the pedagogical issues it raises. Although we shall examine several software programs that are considered by teachers and industry promoters as being exemplary in fostering critical thought, our primary focus will be on how the microcomputer mediates the student's encounter with the symbolic world of culture.

In order to understand how both the inherent technological characteristics of the microcomputer and the person who writes a software program contribute to a particular cultural orientation, we shall have to address the most fundamental questions: What is the nature of technology (i.e., is it neutral)? What is the nature of language? What is the nature of culture? These questions now concern people working to develop computers that are capable of exercising artificial intelligence, but they have not been taken seriously by the advocates and developers of educational software or the devotees of computer literacy—a phrase that designates a form of technical knowledge that would have been more accurately represented as "computer mechanics."

Our approach to laying out the groundwork for putting the microcomputer and the users (writers of software programs, teachers, students) into perspective will involve the use of Gregory Bateson's insight that if we separate an object from its context we are likely to misunderstand it. Meaning and identity evolve from the dynamic nature of the relationships among multiple entities that share (in fact, constitute) the context. Bateson (1974) goes so far as to suggest that the pattern of interrelationship can be understood as a message system—that is, it is a mental process, a form of intelligent activity. Without getting into the revolutionary implications of his cybernetic view of intelligence (he does not associate it with the rationally autonomous individual who acts on the world), it will suffice to keep in mind that we will be considering the microcomputer as part of a context where a number of processes and entities are in continual interaction. Thus we shall be considering how the microcomputer mediates the use of language (what it selects, amplifies, and reduces) in the communication process. The view of language as a conduit for the expression of individual ideas is as widely held as the notion that technology (including the computer) is neutral. But a more recent understanding of how language provides the schemata for organizing thought, a process most clearly seen in the metaphorical nature of thought, raises important questions about the view of language that is incorporated into the microcomputers and the way in which their use in the classroom reinforces in the mind of the student a particular view of language and the world.

After we establish a framework for viewing how language relates to the educational use of microcomputers, attention will be given to how the technology mediates the transmission of culture. Since language and culture are so interwined, it will be possible to move quickly to a consideration of how microcomputers, given the nature of the technology and the ideological orientation of program writers, amplify certain forms of cultural knowledge and value orientations while putting other aspects of culture out of focus. Here we will be concerned with the distinction between explicit and tacit knowledge, the nature of tradition (how it is experienced and how it is mediated by computer technology), and the difference between transmitting culture through the spoken and the written word. Computers are part of the tradition of print technology, and their use in the classroom involves strengthening the thought process and social patterns associated with literacy. By situating the educational use of microcomputers within the current discussion of the differences between orality and literacy, we shall be able to see more clearly why this technology should not be considered as culturally neutral. Lastly, the discussion of microcomputers as amplifiers of certain cultural orientations will focus on more ideological issues. This will involve a consideration of the image of individualism that is reinforced by this print-based technology (which incorporates the conduit view of language). A second ideological issue relates to our cultural way of establishing the authority of our knowledge—particularly the way in which computers strengthen the assumption that objective data give authority to our knowledge claims.

This discussion of the place of microcomputers in the ecology of the classroom—where culture, language, and ideology represent different ways of putting in focus the shared symbolic world—will prepare the ground for a more careful examination of how our cultural blinders cause us to accept at face value the educational claims that are made on behalf of what is represented as the best in educational software. Here we shall take a closer look at the ideological and epistemological questions that should be asked about a data base, Seymour Papert's LOGO, and Tom Snyder's simulation software. This will provide a good test of our new conceptual lenses. The task will be to illuminate how some of the more imaginative software may incorporate cultural mythologies that are dangerous to our collective wellbeing.

The last two chapters of the book will address the clinical (professional) judgments that teachers should be able to exercise about the educational uses of an educational software program, as well as the implications of using microcomputers in the Third World. As the previous chapters will have established that this technology is not culturally neutral, these two chapters will identify what teachers need to be aware of in the technologically mediated process of cultural transmission. The identification of the teacher's responsibility in relation to educational uses of this technology point to the need for teachers in non-Western cultures to understand that the microcomputer is not neutral, that it reinforces a unique configuration of Western beliefs and values. In effect, the need to understand the consequences of using this technology within the context of one's own culture, as well as a sensitivity to the direction of cultural development that is being reinforced, seems to be a universal challenge facing all teachers.

With this overview of the journey ahead, it is time to return to the basic question: Are computers a neutral technology?

CHAPTER 2

Toward a New Understanding of Technology and Language

The early expectation that microcomputers would be widely available for classroom use resulted in a mixed reaction on the part of educators. Some took seriously Seymour Papert's (1980) statement that one of the impacts of the computer would be to make education "more of a private act," thus freeing students from the conservative bureaucracy of the school (p. 37). Although educators did not pick up on Papert's idea that microcomputers would lead to the abandonment of institutionalized learning, they nevertheless urged that school budgeting priorities be changed to reflect the technological revolution that was about to transform the entire educational process. The appointment of computer-education directors and specialists, along with the purchase of microcomputers and software, suggested that this time the promise of fundamental changes in the classroom might actually take place—unlike the failed revolutionary transformations that were envisaged with the introduction of television into the classroom. The transformation of the classroom into a high-tech learning environment was heralded in a score of new journals devoted to advancing the role of microcomputers in education. The new *cause célèbre* within educational circles was the need to spread computer literacy to the entire student population. The recommendation was even made by some computer-education experts that keyboarding should replace cursive writing in the primary grades.

But not all educators viewed the new technology with the same unguarded enthusiasm. Many continued on with the traditional practices of the classroom, yielding only to minor adjustments in classroom routines. Allowing students to participate in a computer lab did not appear as essentially different from attending a physical education class; it was just another expansion of an already crowded curriculum. Others accepted the assigned classroom allotments of machine and software and attempted to integrate drill and practice exercises, word processing, and simulations into the established classroom routine. The momentum for change began to slacken, however, as software and the limited availability of microcomputers led many educators to acknowledge that the introduction of microcomputers had not substantially changed the ambience of most classrooms.

What is of interest to us about this wide range of responses—which still range from unquestioning commitment to achieving the full computerization of the learning process to an attitude that seems to vacillate between stoicism and outright skepticism—is that the most fundamental question about this new technology has never been seriously raised by either the vocal advocates or the teachers who have attempted to articulate their reservations. The question has to do with whether the technology is neutral; that is, neutral in terms of accurately representing, at the level of the software program, the domains of the real world in which people live. If the answer to this question is that it is not neutral, the critically important question of how the technology alters the learning process must then be addressed. Judging the educational significance of this new technology on the basis of the quality of present educational software programs or the future possibility of genuine improvement in this vital area does not seem to be the correct starting point. It is only when the technology is viewed as neutral ("garbage in, garbage out") that the quality of the educational software programs will be the benchmark concern. This misconception of what constitutes the most basic question is likely to continue as long as educators fail to recognize that the microcomputer, along with software programs, is part of the much more complex symbolic world that makes up our culture.

The question of neutrality, as well as the pedagogical and curricular issues surrounding this question, can be put in clearer focus if we *reframe* our way of thinking about microcomputers. But first we need to understand the nature of framing and how it influences the way in which we think and act. Deborah Tannen, a social linguist interested in the role that framing plays in everyday conversational events, gives the example of how the frame of a conversation sets the mood, governs both its content and boundaries, and structures the relationship between the participants. A certain tone of voice may frame the conversation as serious, just as a shift in body language may signal a change in the frame from mutual engagement to a sense that it is time for both participants to pursue other activities (1986). The late sociologist Erving Goffman pointed out that framing not only influences what is deemed the appropriate way of thinking and acting but also provides the markers that set off the activity from the surrounding flow of events (1974). Framing establishes the tenor of a conversation, while also separating it from the surrounding background. But even these boundary lines change, as demonstrated by the manner in which a participant in serious discussion reframes the relationship by telling a joke or drawing attention to a dog that has been narrowly missed by a passing car. Thus reframing changes what we are aware of, as well as our behavior.

One of the most powerful determinants of the frame that governs what will be attended to, and how it will be interpreted, is language. Framing is an aspect of naming. For example, we can now look back on how sexist language framed, at a taken-for-granted level, our way of thinking by constraining what was considered important, how actions were to be interpreted, and what was not considered or seen as relevant—that is, appropriate to the controlling frame. The influence of framing on thought can also be seen in the reference to a guided missile as a "peace-keeper," learning as "behavioral outcomes," and technology as neutral. Language, in providing the initial footing for understanding, establishes the boundaries of the discourse and the interpretative framework that will be viewed as legitimate. Language also provides the basis for reframing—establishing new boundary markers, utilizing a different perspective, legitimating new relationships and values.

For our purposes the process of framing relates to the language and unstated assumptions that have served to regulate how we think about the educational uses of the microcomputer. The frame that established the focus of attention, the language considered appropriate to the importance of the new technology (clear signals were given that only supporters were viewed as competent to speak), and what were perceived as problems that needed to be solved were dictated by people who understood the operational characteristics of the technology. By providing the metaphorical language considered appropriate for thinking about the educational uses of the microcomputer, they controlled the frame that governed the discourse and thus the context for thinking about the educational potential of this new technology. Since the language was derived largely from the technical characteristics of the machine, the question of whether technology is neutral simply fell outside what had been framed as significant to think and talk about. Other important educational, social, and political issues also fell outside the newly defined boundaries of relevance.

My purpose here is to reframe how we think about the educational uses of the microcomputer and, in the process, to establish new conceptual boundaries that take account of the broader cultural consequences of this new technology. As long as we approach the microcomputer in terms of technical and procedural questions (How should we interface the software with the regular curriculum? Can LOGO be used by students to write haiku?), the larger cultural context will be put out of focus.

A basis for reframing how we think about computers is to put in focus one of the most important features of the technology, ironically unnoticed because the traditional framing focused on technical and procedural concerns. What is really unique about the computer is its ability to manipulate symbols in a variety of useful ways. In essence, computers are language-processing machines, a point that is continually emphasized by references to BASIC, Pascal, and FORTRAN as computer languages. The educational software programs are referred to as *written*, and the primary way of relating to the computer is through a keyboard and a video that must be read. Even the much overused and little-understood phrase "computer literacy" suggests the connection of the computer to language usage.

Although the word *literacy* had traditionally meant the ability to decode written symbols, within computer-education circles it became associated with being able to program and, more recently, to operate the machine. One can speculate that the technical challenge of operating an unfamiliar technology may have helped to frame the focus and conceptual boundaries of computer-education experts in a manner that left the question of language, and its connections to thought and culture, outside the boundaries of relevant concern. But the widely held view within our culture that technology is neutral and that language (also a form of technology when expressed in written form) is simply a conduit for the transmission of ideas must also be taken into account when trying to understand why technical and procedural questions have dominated the discourse on the educational uses of the microcomputer. As ironic as it may seem, the educational promoters of this supposedly revolutionary technology appear to have accepted (along with most other groups in society) a view of language and technology that had its roots in the intellectual transformations of the sixteenth and seventeenth centuries (Roszak, 1986; Winograd & Flores, 1986).

The reframing of how we think about the educational uses of the microcomputer should not displace legitimate technical concerns (like the biblical view of the poor, they will always be with us). The shift in focus is intended to open up new areas of thinking that must be used as a context or background for situating the technical concerns (the "how-to" questions). In order to reframe how we think about the computer, from technical questions of how to input and output data to a concern with how the symbol-manipulation processes of computers alter consciousness and reinforce certain cultural orientations, it will be necessary to devote the rest of this chapter to two basic issues: (1) Does technology mediate human experience in a way that reveals its non-neutral character? (2) What are the implications of not accepting the conduit view of language that has its roots in the thinking of John Locke? The next chapter will continue the reframing process for thinking about how microcomputers mediate the educational (cultural transmission) process by taking up a number of issues related to the nature of culture: the nature of tacit knowledge, the political characteristics of language (how language helps to provide a conceptual/political guidance system), the dominant view of tradition and individualism, the shift from ideas to information, and the privileging of literacy over orality (the written over the spoken word). These issues relate to aspects of the cultural milieu within which teachers, students, and microcomputers interact. By reframing our way of understanding in a manner that puts in focus how technology, particularly the software programs, mediates the student's understanding of the symbolic world of culture, it will be easier to recognize the professional judgments that teachers must be able to make, as well as the questions relating to educational goals that remain to be addressed.

IS TECHNOLOGY NEUTRAL?

After listening for several months to local computer-education experts frame discussions on the classroom use of microcomputers in a manner that put their technical skills in focus and my not yet publicly communicated concerns out of focus, I decided to attend a workshop for teachers that was intended to allay their fears about how to fit computers into the traditional patterns of the elementary classroom. One of the most intriguing comments made by the director of the workshop was that the computer was like a pencil: it could be used for either good or bad purposes, depending upon the user. Intrigued by this view of the computer as a neutral technology, I began to pay attention to what other computer-education experts had to say by attending their national conferences and reading their articles and textbooks. Tom Snyder, perhaps one of the most imaginative producers of educational software and a genuinely reflective thinker on the educational implications of this new technology, states in his book (co-written with Jane Palmer) that "in programming the computer is used as a tool-making tool—at its best a 'mind-tool' with which children can invent their *own* intellectual structures and aids to thinking" (1986, p. 98; italics added). The view of the computer as a tool to be utilized by human agency is emphasized in his statement that "the power of the computer is in your hands to do with it as you find best fits your needs and teaching style" (Snyder, no date, p. 25). More recently, Robert McClintock, who is head of the Department of Communication, Computing, and Technology at one of the nation's leading universities, stated that "computers are artifacts, designed and manufactured tools, whereas education is a preeminently cultural phenomenon, something that takes place through and for people" (1988, p. 348). This view of the computer as an neutral tool leads him to make the further claim that "all culture can be coded so it can be operated on with digital computers" (p. 351). Since these statements are based on a number of assumptions that appear to underlie the thinking and practice within the field of educational computing, we shall later return to examine them more closely. For now, we want to keep in focus how computers are viewed as a tool that is culturally neutral.

Textbooks designed for use in university computer-education courses consistently refer to computers as educational tools, with the metaphor of a tool being used to suggest its latent ability to extend the user's power. In being unable to find in educational computing textbooks a discussion of whether the technology is neutral, I often turn to the section where the author lists the most important questions teachers should consider when choosing software. The following is a typical example that reveals the assumptions about the nature of technology; it also serves as an excellent example of how the process of framing puts out of focus the noninstrumental issues associated with this technology. The authors of this particular list, Charles Kinzer, Robert Sherwood, and John Bransford, state that "after the program has been purchased" the teacher should review it by considering the following questions:

1. How can the software be used to improve the instruction program?
2. Can students use the software without teacher assistance?
3. Will students gain the most from this software using it individually or in small groups?
4. Is the content of the software presented accurately?
5. What ability level student can effectively use the program?

6. Is the program compatible with other materials?
7. Is the reading level of the program appropriate? (1986, pp. 185–186)

These questions assume a shockingly low level of professional judgment and common sense on the part of teachers. But more important, they reveal a basic assumption held by most computer-education experts about the nature of technology: namely, that when armed with the right questions teachers will be able to exercise rational judgment about the effective use of this powerful educational tool. Following the image of the pencil wielder, the user (either the teachers, students, or software writer) makes the critical choices, and the technology follows the commands. Abbe Mowshowitz referred to this view of the computer as the "grab bag theory." Metaphorically speaking, "the potential use of the computer is like a grab bag." Individuals are "free to stick their hand into this grab bag and pull out whatever applications they choose." Of course this may require writing new software programs (1984, p. 1).

Even the recent discussion of the computer as a tutor, tool, and tutee reinforces this view of a neutral technology, whose potential simply awaits human direction (Taylor, 1980). The use of the microcomputer as an educational tool that allows students to encounter a conceptual model or to play out a simulation game is evaluated primarily in terms of the educational characteristics of the software program. Similarly, the use of the microcomputer as a tutor (drill and practice exercises) is judged in terms of how it is programmed. The notion of the microcomputer as tutee, where students demonstrate how to use their own understanding as the basis for programming the computer, not only assumes the neutral nature of technology but also incorporates several other cultural misconceptions about the autonomous nature of the individual and the rational process, as well as a conduit view of language (more later about how Papert incorporates all of these misconceptions into his theory of learning).

The view of the neutral nature of technology held by leading spokespersons within the field of educational computing ignores an interesting historical coincidence. In the mid-thirties, when the mathematician and logician A. M. Turing published "On Computable Numbers" (1936), the paper that provided a theoretical framework for understanding the operation of logic machines, Lewis Mumford published *Technics and Civilization* (1934). By focusing on how Western technology (specifically with the introduction of the mechanical clock) had altered consciousness, and thus the patterns of human relationships, Mumford opened up another line of inquiry that was to parallel yet not influence the development of computer technology. This new line of inquiry held that technology should not be understood simply as a tool that serves human interests or as a symbol of progress—a focus of critical concern among nineteenth-century writers.

In the mid-fifties both computer technology and inquiry into the relationship among modern technology, thought, and culture experienced major advances. At a 1956 conference at Dartmouth College a group of mathematicians, psychologists, and electrical engineers exchanged ideas and scholarly papers on how to incorporate into the known capacity of electrical switches the processes associated with human thought. The new field of research that emerged from this conference on using the digital computer to simulate human thought was labeled "artificial intelligence" (AI). Accompanying this new direction in computer research was an unqualified optimism that this new technology would save the human race; as Edward Fredkin, a professor of electrical engineering at MIT, summarized the significance of AI: "It's the question that deals with all questions. In the abstract, nothing can be compared to it. One wonders why God didn't do it. Or, it's a very godlike thing to create a superintelligence, much smarter than we are. It's the abstraction of the physical universe, and this is the ultimate in that direction. If there are any questions to be answered, this is how they'll be answered. There can't be anything of more consequence to happen on this planet" (quoted in McCorduck, 1979, p. 353). Other AI researchers were no less modest in viewing their work as changing the direction of human evolution itself. Geoff Simon, for instance, writes of "emerging computer life forms" that will develop "their own spectrum of feeling, attitudes and emotions" (1985, pp. 133–134).

Several years before the Dartmouth Conference, a German social theorist, Martin Heidegger, and a French philosopher, Jacques Ellul, made major contributions toward understanding how the nature of technology mediates and thus transforms human experience. For thinkers interested in the moral, political, and cultural dangers connected with viewing technology as neutral (or as the embodiment of progress), Heidegger and Ellul provided the ideas that would open up new ways of thinking about the human-technology relationship. Ellul's contribution had the most immediate impact on thinking about technology, although his formulation of the "technological-determinism" argument was so extreme that it was difficult for many to see how to restore to human beings the power to exercise political and moral control over the technological hydra that was not only shaping the direction of our own cultural development but that of other cultures as well.

In 1954, Ellul's *La Technique* (published in English in 1964 under the title, *The Technological Society*) advanced in a massive, detailed argument the thesis that technology, based on the Western assumptions that connected efficiency, control, and rationalism, was now operating according to its own inner logic and had become the dominant force shaping the direction of cultural development around the world. Technology in its premodern state had evolved as a way of compensating for human limitations, but its purpose was to extend and facilitate human skill. Furthermore, it was just one aspect of a culture, limited in use to specific localities. But in its modern form technology operates and evolves according to norms that are beyond human control. Ellul identified these norms as the "automatism of technical choice," "self-augmentation," "monism," and "technical universalism" (1954/1964, pp. 79–147). In explaining the consequences of the modern search for the "one best way" and the desire for "efficient ordering," Ellul observed that "all the business of life, from work and amusement to love and death, is seen from the technical point of view" (p. 117). Ironically, at about the same time that Ellul was identifying how the network of technological innovation had achieved a critical mass where the human task had largely been reduced to performing functions required by technique, the followers of Turing were predicting that by the year 2000 computers would be able to imitate human intelligence perfectly.

Heidegger's thinking about technology was no less encompassing, but his way of approaching the question of what constitutes the "essence of technology in its relationship to human existence" was to be more useful in developing a vocabulary for revealing how our relationships and ways of understanding are framed (the field of possibilities that are established) by the essential nature of technology. According to Heidegger, the essence of technology is existential and thus cannot be viewed simply as a technique that has an independent relationship from the person who uses it. To quote one of his more accessible statements:

> The essence of technology is by no means anything technological. Thus we shall never experience our relationship to the essence of technology so long as we merely conceive and push forward the technological, put up with it, or evade it. Everywhere, we remain unfree and chained to technology, whether we passionately affirm or deny it. *But we are delivered over to it in the worst possible way when we regard it as something neutral;*

> for this conception of it, to which today we particularly like to do homage, makes us utterly blind to the essence of technology. (1954/1977, p. 4; italics added)

Heidegger's reference to the essence of a machine, like a computer, as being "existential" goes against our commonsense understanding. Don Ihde, a particularly insightful interpreter of Heidegger's ideas, has given us a different and more usable set of terms for grasping how technology transforms human experience, or, to use Heidegger's terminology, what constitutes the "essence" of technology. In order to obtain a point of reference for viewing our own culturally conditioned natural attitude that frames our perception of technology as always "ready at hand," waiting to be acted upon, Ihde identifies the characteristics of experience that do not involve the use of technology. His example is that of a person who, standing in an orchard, experiences directly the ripeness, color, taste, and smell of the fruit. It is a direct, unmediated experience. When the individual uses a stick to reach the fruit in the higher branches, the experience is mediated by the essential nature of the technology; that is, the technology transforms qualitatively the nature of the experience. The technology (i.e., the stick) mediates (transforms) the experience by extending the person's reach, while at the same time reducing the ability to touch the fruit (often an essential tactile relationship necessary for determining whether the fruit is ripe) (1979, p. 53).

Ihde uses the terms *amplification* and *reduction* to illuminate how the use of technology transforms our experience. The use of technology, in effect, amplifies certain aspects of human experience and reduces others. The telephone can thus be seen as amplifying our voice over distance while simultaneously reducing our ability to use our own or the other person's body language as part of the message system. The amplification-reduction characteristics of the telephone (amplifying sound while reducing the visual, tactile, and olfactory dimensions of experience) involve what Ihde terms the "selectivity" of technology (1979, p. 56). That is, the essential nature of the technology selects the aspects of experience that will be amplified and reduced. Thus technology is not simply a neutral tool, ready at hand, waiting to be directed by a human being. In effect, it acts on us (through selection and amplification), as we utilize it for our instrumental purposes. Eyeglasses, for example, select and amplify our sense of vision; similarly, the pencil amplifies our ability to record our thoughts in a manner that allows us to achieve distance and view them objectively. The essence of each technology also determines what aspects of experience will be reduced; the pencil, for example, cannot communicate our voice or bring greater acuity to our ability to see or smell.

By asking what it is that the microcomputer selects for amplification and reduction, we can now put in clearer focus what has largely been ignored by the computer-education experts who have incorporated two seemingly incompatible cultural myths into their thinking—that each innovation in computer technology is a further manifestation of social progress, and that technology is inherently neutral. The selection-amplification characteristics of microcomputers are easy to recognize: knowledge that is explicit and can be reduced to discrete bits of data can be stored on a massive scale, manipulated in complex ways that do not distort the sense of accuracy, and recovered in a tireless and efficient manner. These amplification characteristics have been expressed by computer-education experts by the use of such terms as *storage*, *data bases*, and *programming*.

But the reduction characteristics of this technology, which are related both to the essence of the technology and to the cultural mythologies that are written into the software programs, have largely gone unrecognized. Just as the use of the stick reduces the knowledge we obtain by eliminating the sense of touch, and the telephone reduces the messages we communicate by eliminating the use of physical context and body language, the microcomputer also selects out and reduces aspects of experience from the transmission-of-knowledge process that characterizes the educational setting. Since computers function on an algorithmic system, it is impossible to program forms of knowledge that cannot be made explicit and organized into discrete components or whose operational rules cannot be formally represented. Thus the machine that the student interacts with cuts out of the communication process (the reduction phenomenon) tacit-heuristic forms of knowledge that underlie commonsense experience. While the technology amplifies the sense of objectivity, it reduces the awareness that the data represent an interpretation influenced by the conceptual categories and perspective of the person who "collected" the data or information. The technology also reduces the recognition that language, and thus the foundations of thought itself, is metaphorical in nature. The binary logic that so strongly amplifies the sense of objective facts and data-based thinking serves, at the same time, to reduce the importance of meaning, ambiguity, and perspective. Finally, the sense of history, as well as the cultural relativism of both the student's and the software writer's interpretative frameworks, is also put out of focus. As a symbol-processing technology, the computer selects and amplifies certain aspects of language; ironically, the form of knowledge that is encoded in the form of language suited to this technology represents the positivism of the nineteenth century (Bowers, 1988).

This process of cultural selection, amplification, and reduction can be seen occurring in any educational software program, as the language of the program serves to frame conceptually what is to be represented to the student. We shall look briefly at two examples of software programs that select for amplification a particular set of cultural values. The first is a simulation program called *Oh, Deer!* Its purpose is to provide students with the opportunity to simulate the decision-making process of solving the social and ecological problems associated with a deer population that has outgrown the carrying capacity of the habitat. In addition to role-playing situations, the program provides a wealth of information and data on the reproductive characteristics and environmental impact of deer. As the producers of the program put it, "students get a chance to experiment with the many variables affecting the mathematical model of a deer herd" (Minnesota Educational Computing Consortium, 1983, p. 1).

Culturally, what the program selects for amplification is the technological mind-set that reduces problem solving to a matter of basing social-policy decisions on data. The amplification of a specific cultural orientation to solving problems by gathering data involves, at the same time, selecting out of the communication process the importance of considering the underlying cultural assumptions that frame people's perceptions and use of the land, what constitutes the "cost-efficiency of management methods," and their own resource-depletion habits. For all of its educational strengths, and there are many, the program fails to address the deeper cultural patterns of thought and behavior that are an integral part of the problem of ecological imbalance students are to resolve. Instead, students encounter the one-dimensional world of objective data. The deeper cultural patterns of thought that are not made explicit by the person who created the software can be seen by comparing the technicist orientation of the program, where humans are viewed as the only source of intelligent behavior, with Gregory Bateson's argument that the tradition of thought that locates intelligence within the individual leads to ecological disaster. The individual, as part of a larger ecology of relationships, participates in the mental characteristics (or message exchanges) of the entire system. If the entire ecosystem is to survive, as Bateson points out, the technicist view of the environment as mindless must undergo radical change (1974).

A second example of educational software represents a response to a popular simulation program, *Oregon Trail,* that was perceived as amplifying a masculine interpretation of the pioneer experience. In an attempt to engage female students, as well as compensate for the bias in gender orientation of the *Oregon Trail, Jenny of the Prairie* was designed as a simulation program that involves a young girl exercising the skills and judgments required for surviving alone on the pioneer trail. In addition to asking students to make decisions about building a shelter, gathering food, and dealing with wild animals (with each decision worth a different number of points), the designers of the program select for amplification a cultural value that fits more properly with today's relativistic orientation than it does with cultural patterns that characterized Jenny's time. The problematic situations students are to solve, as they re-enact the pioneer experiences of Jenny, involve rewarding "experimentation, with no 'right' or 'wrong' answers," as the designers of the program put it (Rhiannon Software, 1984, p. 12).

The representation of decision making as the expression of individual imagination, entirely untainted by the influence of cultural analogues, raises an important question about whether historical accuracy should be sacrificed in order to promote a more liberated set of values. But more germane to our discussion of how educational computing involves the process of cultural selection, amplification, or reduction is the representation of the decision maker (Jenny) as free of cultural influences. The attempt to compensate for the lack of gender balance in the *Oregon Trail* led the designers to go far beyond the presentation of a strong feminist image for students to identify with. The reinforcement of the view that *all* decisions should be viewed as experimental and thus relative makes the new program as problematic, though in a different way, as the one it was to replace.

The point might be made that all educational software will involve the amplification of certain cultural values and ways of thinking and that this process will, by necessity, lead to the omission of other aspects of culture. After all, so the argument might go, developing educational software shares the basic problem of language in that not everything can be represented at the same time. This response to my argument is, in part, correct; but it represents an insight that has generally not been taken seriously within the field of educational computing—partly because thinking about educational computing has been framed in a manner that has put out of focus the importance of understanding how deeply experience is embedded in culture. But there is a more fundamental reason why these two software programs amplify the view of individuals as autonomous decision makers who base the rational process on either objective information or, more romantically conceptualized, on direct experience. According to Terry Winograd and Fernando Flores (1986), computer technology is based on the Cartesian view of knowledge; since one of the characteristics of this tradition is to deal only with the explicit and observable aspects of experience, the people writing the educational software have tended to ignore the tacit dimension of our cultural-linguistic experience. It would also be fair to say that the designers of educational software, in not being aware of the phenomenological traditions of thought, have simply ignored the epistemological problem of how to represent the cultural foundations of a person's tacit knowledge, which is highly contextual, through a media that decontextualizes knowledge and can only deal with what is known at an explicit level of awareness. If Winograd and Flores are correct in their analysis of the limitations of the computer as a Cartesian machine (Theodore Roszak, 1986, makes a similar argument in *The Cult of Information*), the problem of representing the tacit, contextual, and metaphorical dimensions of cultural experience in educational software programs will not be resolved by designing new programs, like *Jenny of the Prairie*, that address new and highly politicized concerns. The dynamics of cultural selection, amplification, and reduction will continue, partly because of the characteristics of the technology, partly because of the unexamined assumptions of the designer of the educational software, and partly because of the widespread belief within the field of educational computing that technology is neutral. It is to be hoped that developing a conceptual framework for making explicit how the culture is mediated through the process of educational computing, as well as the specific cultural orientations that are reinforced by this technology, will make it possible to give more serious thought to the problem.

Scholars interested in the politics of language and ideology have provided alternative perspectives to that of Heidegger and Ihde for viewing the non-neutral nature of technology and thus the way in which educational computing contributes to the current cultural crisis of privileging an instrumental form of thinking. Jürgen Habermas, a leading Critical Theory philosopher, observed that "technics, as a universe of instrumentalities, may increase the weakness as well as the power of man. At the present stage, he is perhaps more powerless over his own apparatus than he ever was before" (1971, p. 89). The reason Habermas viewed technology as a new source of oppression relates to the way modern technology has been invested with an ideological (i.e., political) orientation. Of special concern is the way in which technology reinforces a purposive rational mode of thought—an orientation toward instrumental problem solving, efficiency in the control of pre-figured outcomes, and the reduction of experience to measurable outcomes. "Today," Habermas warned, "domination perpetuates and extends itself not only through technology, but *as* technology" (p. 84).

The "rationalization" of society, and thus the spread of an instrumental ideology through technological development, is manifested, in part, through basic changes in our thought processes that occur as we borrow from our technologies the metaphors that direct (frame) our thought. The substitution of the word *information* (which computers process) for the word *ideas* suggests, according to Theodore Roszak (1986), a critically important shift in our worldview toward a more technicist political agenda. The conflating of computer memory with human memory also troubles him. Representing thinking as "information retrieval" and machines as capable of "artificial intelligence" are further examples of how technology can become the source of such power that it alters the metaphorical foundations of our symbolic world.

The evocative nature of certain forms of technology, such as the mechanical clock, print, and now computers, has altered our language usage in other ways. Scholars such as Walter Ong (1977, 1982) and Jack Goody (1977) have recently directed attention to how print (a tradition further strengthened by computer technology) reinforces a different form of thinking and social relationship than is associated with the spoken word. Since we shall later take a closer look at the implications of their analysis of the difference between the spoken and written word, we shall conclude here with an observation made by the French philosopher Jean-François Lyotard on how the growing computerization of society is transforming both the nature of knowledge and the social processes associated with its transmission. While not using Ihde's metaphors of amplification and reduction, Lyotard views the computer as a culturally and politically transforming technology. As he puts it, "the nature of knowledge cannot survive unchanged" within a social context characterized by the proliferation of information-processing machines. The nature of knowledge, if it is to fit into the technology and become operational, must be translated into quantities of information (1984, p. 16). McClintock's statement about translating "the stuff of culture into binary code" (1988, p. 351), which is based on a set of assumptions shared by others in the field of educational computing, represents the very problem Lyotard is alerting us to. Not only does Lyotard view this growing emphasis on "knowledge in the form of an informational commodity indispensable to productive power" as leading to a different and dangerous new form of worldwide competition for power, he also sees a profound social change occurring as the narrative form of knowledge is undermined by the more "scientific" form that can be processed through the computer and communicated through print. The narrative tradition, he writes, "is also the tradition of the criteria defining a threefold competence—'knowing how,' 'knowing how to speak,' and 'knowing how to hear'—through which the community's relationship to itself and its environment is played out. What is transmitted through these narratives is the set of pragmatic rules that constitute the social bond" (1984, p. 21).

The narrative form involves a mutual re-enactment of the community of memory, providing the analogues for guiding human experience as well as a deep sense of psychological involvement in an ongoing and vital community. It is, at the same time, the thread that connects individual memory to the more collective memory that extends into the past. Thus the narrative form of knowledge is essential to constituting a sense of self-identity as a communal being. Unlike information, the narrative form of knowledge strengthens the sense of relationship.

This brief summary of issues that come into view as we explore the simple question of whether technology is neutral suggests the need for a drastic reframing of the boundaries for thinking about the educational uses of microcomputers. The reframing of what should be encompassed by the idea of computer literacy should also take into account a second basic misconception upon which computer technology, including software programs, is based—namely, that language is a conduit for transmitting information. We shall now take up this question as well as the educational issues that surround a technology that incorporates this myth.

IMPLICATIONS OF VIEWING LANGUAGE AS A CONDUIT

In *Mind Storms*, Seymour Papert lays out the epistemological foundations for LOGO, a computer language that allows students to explore the structure of an idea by conceptualizing its modular characteristics (i.e., component parts). As part of his justification for a computer language that shifts to the student the power to control the program, and thus to "think about thinking," Papert makes an insightful observation about the nature of language: "A programming language is like a natural language in that it favors certain metaphors, images, and ways of thinking" (1980, p. 34). After admonishing educators for not paying "attention to the choice of language," and establishing to his own satisfaction the educational advantages of a programming language that supposedly facilitates student control over the cognitive process, Papert drops the issue.

As an examination of the literature of the field will reveal, language appears to be totally nonproblematic except in terms of the need to increase the student's skills in using the computer to communicate information more effectively. If Papert's comment on the hidden complexity of language is the exception, the following statement by Henry Jay Becker can be taken to represent the norm for thinking about communication (people in the field tend to conflate language and communication):

> Because the purpose of schooling is to prepare students for the world after schooling, instruction should relate to intellectual activities that will be predominant in society a decade or so ahead. For example, interpersonal communication is not only increasingly written rather than verbal, it is also increasingly based on typed or machine-retrievable printed text rather than handwritten text. In addition, keyboard communication will be for the near future the primary means of man-machine communication as well. Thus, the teaching of typing skills may be reasonably regarded as a basic academic skill that should be learned as early as such skills become useful in the context of education or extra-curricular life. (1983, p. 37)

The distinction that interests Becker, and it is only a superficial one, is between verbal and written language, with the latter being associated with social and technological progress. His real concern is insuring that "the more rapidly and effortlessly that students can translate what *they want to say* to the computer in machine readable communication, the more effective will be the time spent at the computer station" (p. 37; italics added). Language (or communication) appears simply as the medium for transmitting what "they want to say." The writings of other computer-education experts similarly take language for granted, perceiving it as undeserving of special attention because it is like the other "neutral" technologies we use.

Language is indeed a technology in that it involves the formalizing of sounds and syntactical rules that enable people to communicate with each other. Printed language reveals even more directly the connection with technology; in its earliest form the crude markings that were the precursors of the alphabet were used as a technique for aiding in the memory of business transactions and military logistics. The issue for us to consider is not whether language is viewed by computer-education experts as another instance of a neutral technology (their continual references to language in instrumental terms give away their attitude of taking language for granted). A more important concern relates to the educational consequences of using microcomputers in a manner that reinforces the view that language is a conduit for the communication of information and ideas. Although it was unnecessary to do so in the previous discussion of how to illuminate the amplification and reduction characteristics of a technology, here we need to approach the non-neutral nature of language, and thus challenge the image of language serving a conduit function, in terms of a different vocabulary and set of concepts. In effect we need to situate (frame) this form of technology within the context of our symbolic world in order to clarify the language-thought connection that educators need to understand more fully. We must also keep in mind that the view of language being criticized here is widely held in our society and is continually reinforced in educational settings ranging from kindergarten through graduate school.

The metaphorical language associated with computers—input, output, storage, memory, retrieval, and so forth—is based on an image of data and information being inputed into the computer and stored until a person wants to retrieve it (often after performing certain manipulations). The input-output model has as its internal connecting link a transmission process. This view of language as the conveyor or conduit through which the "inputs" and "outputs" are transmitted is clearly illustrated in this more sophisticated view of the technological capabilities of the computer:

> Although the computer stores information and presents it to students just as books and films do, and although it can only do the four simple tasks of accepting input of information, storing it, manipulating it, and providing output, the computer:
>
> 1. Stores its information in a fluid, electronic matrix, so that it can be held in reserve and presented to the student in any order—not just from beginning to end.
> 2. Is interactive, so that the student can put in information as well as receive it.
> 3. Can combine the potentials of fluid information storage and interactive ability to deliver the information its program contains contingent upon the student's input. (Siegal & Davis, 1986, p. 24)

That this imputing and storing of information is dependent upon the use of metaphorical language that provides the schemata for organizing thought is put out of focus by this statement. Another typical example of viewing language as a conduit is illustrated in the statement by Alfred Bork, an expert on applying the computer to the thinking of physics, who writes about the "student's input and how the system accepts the input" (Taylor, 1980, p. 33). Papert relies upon a similar metaphorical image of ideas being conveyed through inputs but, in terms of LOGO, this involves the use of the Turtle as conveying agent:

> Thus teaching the turtle to act or "think" can lead one to reflect on one's own actions and thinking. And as children move on, they program the computer to make more complex decisions and find themselves engaged in reflecting on more complex aspects of their own thinking. (1980, p. 28)

For Papert, the key is having students become sensitive to what it is they have *conveyed* through the turtle (which provides access to the LOGO language system). The examples that represent language as a medium through which information is transmitted are as numerous as the books and articles written on the uses of computers in education. More important, the literature appears to contain *no* counterexamples for how to think about language.

The conduit view of language used by computer-education experts and writers of instructional software programs is further buttressed by the view of individualism and the nature of the rational process that they hold. Individuals are represented as autonomous beings who possess the power of agency; that is, they can initiate inputs, retrieve data, and so forth. Similarly, the rational process involves a reflective activity that occurs within the head of individuals and is represented as a process over which they exercise control. These assumptions about the attributes of the individual are especially important because in order to continue to believe in them one has to hold, at the same time, the assumption that language is a conduit through which the ideas, information, and data generated by the rational activity of the individual can be transmitted to other rational and autonomous individuals (what gets sent through the conduit of language then serves as an expansion of the data base for the other person's thought process). If language is viewed as non-neutral—that is, as a dynamic process that shapes our thoughts as we use it to communicate with others—we would be forced to rethink our view of the autonomous individual and the rational process as free of cultural influence. We shall later take up the implications of a more culturally and linguistically grounded view of the individual and the rational process for how we think about the educational uses of the microcomputer. For now it is important to examine more closely why the conduit view of language must be understood as a basic misconception.

In a seminal article, "The Conduit Metaphor—A Case of Frame Conflict in Our Language About Language," Michael Reddy puzzles about the view of language represented in such typical utterances as "It is very difficult to put this concept *into* words," "It's very hard to get that idea *across*," "Never *load* a sentence with more than it can carry," "His words *carry* little in the way of recognizable meaning" (1979, pp. 321–23). If one were to take a tape recorder into a classroom these examples could be duplicated many times over. The metaphorical image of language as a conduit, where concepts are put *into* words and words are expected to *carry* meaning to others, reflects a number of assumptions that appear in four general categories of expression:

> (1) Language functions like a conduit, transforming thoughts bodily from one person to another; (2) in writing and speaking, people insert their thoughts or feelings into the words; (3) words accomplish the transfer by containing the thoughts or feelings and conveying them to others; and (4) in listening or reading, people extract the thoughts and feelings once again from the words. (p. 290)

As Reddy points out, if this view of language were correct (i.e., "that information is *contained* in a transmitted message") learning would be effortless and accurate. It would be like believing that "communication is a 'success without effort' system," (1979, p. 308). The problem with this view of language is that learning would be viewed as overly passive, with the learner simply taking in ideas and information conveyed by language. This sender-receiver model of learning, with language serving as the connecting conduit, introduces several basic errors in understanding the nature of knowledge and the dynamic interplay between language and thought.

The sender-receiver model of thought and communication (or input-output, to stay with the jargon associated with computers) reinforces the view that the ideas, information, and data that are transmitted through language are objective. That is, the human authorship of the knowledge is obscured. What moves through the conduit of language takes on the appearance of objectivity. This view is clearly represented in the previously quoted statement by Martin Siegel and Dennis Davis that the computer performs the "task of accepting input of information, storing it, manipulating it, and providing output" (1986, p. 24). Another example of the conduit view of language, with its concomitant of objective knowledge, is contained in a warning given by Fay Wheeler about the use of a data base:

> If you decide to use databases in your classroom, remind your students that the warning "Don't believe everything you read" holds as true for databases as it does for books. Databases, like any collection of factual materials, may contain blatant inaccuracies; perhaps someone typed in a wrong number or collected data in a haphazard manner. (1987, p. 32)

The interactive language of the microcomputer is represented as the conduit through which the objective information (or haphazardly collected data) flows. But according to Reddy, as well as others informed by the sociology of knowledge, this view of objective knowledge and its transmission misrepresents how knowledge is humanly constructed over time in culturally specific ways and continually reconstructed as it is communicated to others.

The use of such metaphorical expressions as *discovering knowledge, finding knowledge,* and *storing knowledge* belong to the "keep your eyes open and your mind receptive" school of thought. By way of contrast, the constructionist perspective recognizes that the individual views the world through an interpretative framework or schema that is acquired through the socialization process. This interpretative framework includes the conceptual categories and assumptions shared by other members of the language community. As Benjamin Lee Whorf put it:

> Formulation of ideas is not an independent process, strictly rational in the old sense, but is part of a particular grammar, and differs, from slightly to greatly, between different grammars. We dissect nature along lines laid down by our native languages. The categories and types that we isolate from the world of phenomena we do not find there because they stare every observer in the face; on the contrary, the world is presented in a kaleidoscopic flux of impressions which has to be organized by our minds—and this means largely by the linguistic systems in our minds. We cut nature up, organize it into concepts, and ascribe significances as we do, largely because we are parties to an agreement to organize it in this way—an agreement that holds throughout our speech community and is codified in the patterns of our language. The agreement is, of course, an implicit and unstated one, *but its terms are absolutely obligatory*; we cannot talk at all except by subscribing to the organization and classification of data which the agreement decrees. (1968, pp. 324–25)

Although the unique elements in each individual's pattern of socialization contribute to important variations in perspective and interpretation (Ward Goodenough referred to this as the individual's own "idiolect"; 1981, p. 32), the cultural episteme, mediated through personal experience, leads to the construction rather than discovery of knowledge. According to Reddy, language provides symbolic templates used to express what is understood by individuals, given their respective interpretative-existential frameworks. Similarly, other participants in the communication process are not passive recipients of somebody else's discoveries; they are also involved in the interpretation (co-construction) process. In fact, communication is only possible because of the shared symbolic templates that are acquired as one becomes a member of a speech community.

When we ignore how participants replay the message to fit the conceptual-existential framework they bring to it, we then have a myth that represents knowledge as independent of human beings. "In its simplest terms," Reddy prophetically warned, "the conduit metaphor lets human ideas slip out of human brains, so that once you have recording technologies, you do not need humans anymore" (1979, p. 310). But it is not just another garden-variety myth that is more nuisance than real threat; it seems to have captured the imagination of people who do, in fact, view human beings as irrelevant to the new world of *Machina sapiens* that is emerging. Geoff Simon quotes approvingly Kevin Ulmer, who, as director of exploratory research for Genex Company, observed that the "ultimate scenario is to develop a complete genetic code for the computer that would function as a virus does, but instead of producing more virus, it would assemble a fully operational computer inside a cell." Simon notes approvingly that "in this way a biological computer could be made to propagate itself, possibly with modifications to allow for evolutionary progress" (1985, p. 207). *Machina sapiens* would then have no need for *Homo sapiens*, which is a way of thinking that has its roots in a view of knowledge and language that omits the importance of human beings and culture.

In addition to the conduit view of language being undermined by the recognition that knowledge is an ongoing interpretation, reflecting the perspectives and cultural conditioning (used in the weak sense of the term) of the participants, Reddy makes another point about the nature of language itself that further undermines the sender-receiver model. His own analysis of the consequences of using a "conduit metaphor" as a basis for thinking about language illuminates how language itself is metaphorical. Instead of viewing language as a neutral transmitter of thought, whereby we put our meanings, ideas, and information into words (i.e., empty vessels waiting to be filled and transmitted to others), the recognition of the metaphorical nature of language leads to an awareness of how language helps to organize and direct the process of thinking itself. As Donald A. Schon (1979) put it, the use of language to name a situation or relationship also frames the context we will use to think about it. Thus naming is a form of framing; that is, it establishes the conceptual boundaries and provides the template or model for thinking.

Before we use the metaphorical nature of language as a way of illuminating the non-neutrality of language (how "language speaks" us, to quote Heidegger, 1982, p. 124), it is important to obtain a fuller understanding of metaphorical thinking. The German philosopher, Friedrich Nietzsche was one of the first to recognize that we cannot entirely understand the new on its own terms; "in *our* thought," he wrote, "the essential feature is fitting new material into old schemas . . . making equal what is new" (1888/1968, p. 273). Stated in more contemporary terms, "the essence of metaphor is understanding and experiencing one kind of thing in terms of another" (Lakoff & Johnson, 1980, p. 5). The technological capacity of the computer to store data could have been called *flug*, but few people would have understood this characteristic of computers. The use of the word *memory* enables people to think of computers as having characteristics that are similar to what is already understood about certain features of the human mind. Thus the new is understood in terms of the already familiar—as Nietzsche suggests.

This process of understanding the new in terms of the familiar (which often involves comparisons between entities from different domains), as well as rethinking the familiar in terms of new developments, represents the analogic form of metaphorical thinking. Comparing computers with human intelligence, and now with life itself (Geoff Simon writes that "computers can be seen as emerging life forms"; 1985, p. 133), is an example of the former; taking an old and tired image such as that of the classroom and revitalizing it by thinking of it as like a high-powered, data-based management process is an example of the latter form of analogic thinking. After the analogic form of thinking establishes (frames) how we are to think of the new, we move beyond the deliberate phase of thinking of something as being like something else and into the taken-for-granted use of iconic metaphors, where the basis of the comparison is highlighted and frozen into an image word that provides the new sense of understanding. The following statement on genetic engineering contains a number of iconic (image) metaphors that are now self-referencing in the sense that we do not have to ask about what is meant by the use of the word: "One of the biologist's most important tools for tinkering with genes is a set of chemical 'scissors' called restriction enzymes" (Cowen, 1986, p. 18). We already know about *tools, tinkering,* and *scissors;* by carrying over from other contexts understandings that can be applied to new situations, we advance our ability to grasp the new by embedding it in the familiar. But the framing of how we should think is now internalized in the iconic metaphor (e.g., *classroom management, computer literacy, information storage, individualized instruction, student as product,* and so forth). Other iconic metaphors, such as *intelligence, individualism, data,* and *frame,* reproduce in thought the assumptions and ways of thinking that characterize the social context from which they were derived. Thus when we use iconic metaphors in a taken-for-granted manner, our thought is being largely organized by the framing characteristics of the metaphor. For example, *individualism* suggests for most middle-class people the sense of being autonomous and self-directing; the image puts out of focus the spatial-social context as well as the culture that has been internalized.

There is another level to how language helps frame how we think. Underlying such statements as "your claims are indefensible," "his criticisms were right on target," and "he shot down all my arguments" is what Schon calls a "generative metaphor" that organizes thinking, in terms of this example, about how an argument is an expression of warfare (1979, p. 254). A generative, or root, metaphor provides the most basic conceptual template or paradigm, not only influencing the selection of iconic (image) metaphors but also providing the most basic conceptual patterns for organizing thought. Schon uses the example of how the generative metaphor of *blight* and *disease* led urban planners to think in terms of a more total approach ("removal") to slum clearance; thinking of the slum as a *natural community,* on the other hand, led to thinking about strengthening existing "informal networks," "patterns of interaction," and "spatial identity." Other generative, or root, metaphors include a mechanistic view of society, a view of technology as neutral, and a conduit view of language—to use examples germane to the issues we are addressing.

The generative metaphor provides the basic conceptual framework that shapes our interpretation, provides a sense of coherence among images, and dictates what iconic metaphors will be appropriate. For example, the computer is now becoming a model (generative metaphor) for thinking about the mental processes of the individual; when our thought is guided by this model it makes perfectly good sense to substitute *data base* for *memory, retrieval* for *recall,* and *input* for *communicate*. When using the computer as a paradigm for thinking about mental processes, it seems inappropriate to associate memory with the personal aspects of a life history (feelings, the darker aspects that are repressed, and so forth), recall with intentionality and a sense of moral responsibility, and communication with meaning. As computers have not yet "evolved" to the point envisioned by Geoff Simon, associating computers with personal experience, feelings, existential choice, responsibility, and so forth does not seem to make sense. Consistency, as dictated by the generative metaphor, requires that only image metaphors suggesting machine-like capabilities be used. Similarly, the generative metaphor that pictures language as a conduit cannot encompass the idea that "language speaks us" or that language is metaphorical in nature. Either idea requires a different generative metaphor or paradigm, which will, in turn, lead to a different way of thinking about the nature of the individual and the rational process.

With religion no longer providing an overarching root metaphor, we seem to be creating a host of minor ones and revising older ones as we go along. Feminism led to rethinking those aspects of the cultural paradigm where inequality was part of a commonsense view of human relationships. But new generative metaphors that represent human experience as a system that can be engineered seem to be gaining adherents; thus we have a whole new set of iconic metaphors that represent the student as a product, the curriculum as a delivery system, and the mind as something that can be programmed. The important point here, as Schon argues, is that our collective past and ongoing cultural experiences provide the symbolic basis for the generative and iconic metaphors that frame our way of understanding and communicating.

The conduit view of language and the accompanying view of the thought process have significant implications for the person who writes the instructional software program, as well as for the teacher and students who use it. An example taken from a discussion by John F. Wedman on "Making Software More Useful" provides a useful reference point for grasping the full significance of the current blindness toward language that characterizes the field. This example is particularly useful because it represents a conscious effort to provide classroom teachers with guidelines that will enable them to identify and supplement the deficiencies of an instructional software program. The basic problem, as Wedman understands it, is to "(1) identify the instructional functions provided by the program; and (2) supply those that are missing." Deficiencies in a program could be determined by judging it in terms of the nine "events of instruction" that he lists: (1) gaining attention, (2) informing learner of objectives, (3) stimulating recall of prerequisites, (4) presenting stimuli, (5) providing guidance, (6) eliciting performance, (7) providing feedback, (8) assessing performance, and (9) enhancing retention and transfer. If a software program fails to provide for any of these "events of instruction," the teacher should "then select the appropriate strategies for complementing the software" (1986, p. 11).

In contrast to Wedman's concerns, which have to do with instructional procedures and not with the educational content of the program, we find that an awareness of the influence of language on thought leads to asking a different set of questions. His position assumes objectivity in the representation, transmission, and internalization of knowledge—all of which are predicated on a conduit view of language. Since the person who creates the educational software uses a natural language to communicate with the student, the language must also be understood as metaphorical in nature. This basic point applies to data bases, simulations, and even to LOGO. The language, whether in sentence form or single words, includes both iconic and generative metaphors. At the most basic level of significance, the naming process that the programmer is taking the student through (what can be termed "primary socialization" when the student is encountering an explanation of some aspect of the culture for the first time) is also a framing process—to go back to Schon's insight. That is, the metaphorical images, when shared by the communication process, will provide the footing for shared understanding while at the same time establishing the boundaries that separate the relevant (as dictated by the metaphor) from the irrelevant.

An example of how words, as iconic metaphors, frame the student's way of understanding can be seen in how the pioneers, in an early version of *Oregon Trail*, are represented as being attacked by "bandits." This is a powerful image metaphor that most students already understand, but by framing the students' understanding of the westward movement of the pioneers through the use of this metaphor the programmer puts out of focus (deframes) the fact that the pioneers were displacing other cultural groups and that the "bandits" were actually indigenous peoples who were struggling to protect their homeland and lifestyle from foreign invaders. The naming of states and territories (like Oregon) also serves to frame how students will understand the most basic relationships. Reference to the Oregon Territory establishes our own historical relationship with this part of the continent, while hiding the fact that other inhabitants understood the territory in terms of a more regional set of names—Shoshone, Nez Perce, Umatilla, Klamath, and so forth. Furthermore, if the end of the Oregon Trail were represented as the valley of the Kalapuya and Molalla, rather than Portland and Oregon City (the names given by the European settlers and explorers), students might be prompted to view the westward migration as more complex than the settlement of an empty wilderness by the rugged and courageous pioneers who were, as the metaphor suggests, the first to open the land for others. The land had already been occupied for thousands of years; consequently the image of a pioneer, like our perception of the history of the territory (which is framed by being given a Western name), distorts and obfuscates the clash of cultures that was occurring. For students who view themselves as engaged in a simulation of critical decision making about how to expend limited resources in order to succeed in traversing an unfriendly wilderness, there are no warnings or guidelines for the trip they will take through the mind-set of the person who wrote the software program. In the re-enactment of these historical events, fact, fiction, myth, greed, deceit, and courage are all mixed together. Given the fact that computer simulations represent a process of socialization to a particular way of thinking, it is important to emphasize that Wedman's suggestion for recognizing the limitations of instructional software programs will not help either teacher or students recognize that the most critical issue is the failure to assess the adequacy of how language is used to frame how they understand their own experience and that of others.

In case the reader is thinking I have chosen a weak software program to make a point that otherwise would not stand up, the preceding discussion of the metaphorical nature of language can just as well be related to Tom Snyder's game of global conflict resolution, *The Other Side* (1985a). This sophisticated exercise in strategic decision making, where the students (players) have to balance domestic with international interests, competition with cooperation, peace with war, involves communication between members of two nations. The decision makers representing the two sides must communicate through a "hot line" that severely restricts the information that can be exchanged. Thus the problem of assessing the assumptions and guessing the intended strategy of the other side forces students to think hard and clearly about the basis for their own decisions. Yet for all its complexity, this simulation in decision making that is supposed to keep the C.A.D. (computer-assisted defense) on each side from imposing a military solution reflects the mentality of the technocrat who sees in all cultures the same basic elements—technology, economy, and strategic resources. For example, the possible categories of action for members, regardless of which side they are on, are "build, run mixer, tank repair, inspection, prospecting, number sheet, exchange, attack, fuel gift, money gift, cease fire zone, underground" (Snyder, 1985b, p. 20).

Although Snyder states that "communications between nations are always subject to the problems which arise from misunderstandings, ambiguities and mistrust," the language possessed by the members of the two sides frames the same view of reality. But it is not a view that takes account of the symbolic foundations of a culture that provides its members, to quote Clifford Geertz, "the tone, character, and quality of their life, its moral and aesthetic style and mood—and their world view—the picture they have of the way things in sheer actuality are, their most comprehensive ideas of order" (1973, p. 89).

The cultural assumptions that Snyder builds into *The Other Side* represent the individual as a rational decision maker who only needs information about economic, technological, and military variables. But culture, as Geertz and other anthropologists understand it, is a factor that has to be taken into account in understanding the basis of decision making. For example, in the resource guide designed to help teachers maximize the benefits of the learning game, Snyder suggests that as a pregame option relating to the establishment of a sense of national identity "each team [could] create a name, flag, and national characteristic for its country" (1985b, p. 10). These visible manifestations of group identity are really superficial when compared to the cultural forms encoded in the vocabulary of a language community. But it is the latter that has the most profound influence on the values and pattern of thinking that underlie the decision-making process that the students are to simulate.

As an example, the word *compromise* has a very different meaning for Americans than it has for Britons; similarly, our view of individualism is very different from that of the Japanese. At a more fundamental level, Ron and Suzanne Scollon, two social linguists who have worked extensively with Athabaskan language groups, report that in Koyukon the subject and object of an action are represented as a joint activity. "In the Koyukon grammar you shoot 'with' a lynx in the same way that in English you go to the corner drugstore with a friend. It is something the two of you do together" (1985, pp. 16–17). To cite another example, English speakers are accustomed to counterfactual thinking, wherein such phrases as "if-then," "what if," and "suppose this were to be considered" lead to considering a state of affairs that is known to be theoretical and speculative. In fact, considering the implications of a hypothetical situation is exactly what *The Other Side* requires. Alfred Bloom, a linguist who has investigated the differences in cognitive repertoires between the English and Chinese, reports that the

> Chinese language has no distinct lexical, grammatical, or intentional device to signal entry into the counterfactual realm, to indicate explicitly that the events referred to have definitely not occurred and are being discussed for the purpose only of exploring the might-have-been or the might-be. (1981, p. 52)

In addition to how different languages help structure experience, there are even cultural differences in how silence is viewed. Ron Scollon reports that among the Chipewyans of Northern Alberta "quiet is a term for knowledge, control, cooperation, attention to others, and a socially productive attitude" (1985, p. 27). Suppose a group of Fort Chipewyan students were hooked up to play *The Other Side* with a group of students from the Bronx, New York. Given the differences in how these two cultural groups (assuming a certain ethnic homogeneity of the Bronx students) use pauses (silence) in their conversational style, it is easy to imagine that ignorance of the cultural processes at work could lead the quicker group of students (in terms of a faster pace of communication) to make stereotyped inferences about the slow group that would, in turn, lead to miscalculations and misinterpretations. The causes of political disasters in the adult world can often be traced back to the failure to recognize the cultural differences in cognitive and communicative styles; and *The Other Side,* in spite of its technological sophistication, fails to address this longstanding problem.

The reader may now be thinking that I should accept *The Other Side* for what it is and not criticize it for not dealing with the linguistic and cultural factors. But my point is that it fails to fulfill the promise of its creators (to teach "the dynamics of peace and global conflict resolution") by ignoring how the language of a cultural group influences the decision-making process. Snyder's software program, in effect, will reinforce in the minds of the participants the conduit view of language (i.e., they put their decisions into words and communicate them to the other side), as well as a view of the rational process that does not take into account how culture provides the symbolic foundations (generative metaphors) that guide and shape the thought process of its members.

As the discussion up to this point indicates, there are real dangers in framing our thinking about the educational uses of microcomputers in a way that puts out of focus the dynamic interplay of culture, language, and thought. The people who work with the instructional software, as well as the teacher who guides its use in the classroom, need to understand that the language they are using is not neutral. In addition to its metaphorical nature, language must be understood as having a history that is reproduced in our consciousness (e.g., our use of the word *intelligence* reproduces in thought the assumptions and pattern of thinking of the historical period from which it was originally derived). Language also provides a conceptual guidance system that not only helps to frame how we think but also establishes the boundaries and what we will tend to pay attention to within these boundaries. This conceptual guidance system can also be understood as a political guidance system, since what we are able to think about guides the choices we will see as open.

The previous statement hints at an important issue that has generally been ignored by the experts concerned with software evaluation and what has come to be called the "classroom application" of microcomputers; that is, that the classroom use of the microcomputer involves the student in a process of political socialization. Without using the technical vocabulary, we have been dealing with questions of how knowledge and power interrelate. The amplification-reduction characteristics of a technology, as well as the conduit view of language (and the counterarguments about its metaphorical nature), can be understood as expressions of the knowledge-power connection. But in order to explicate this more fully and to explore its educational implications, it will be necessary to turn to a fuller consideration of the characteristics of culture that are not amplified by the classroom use of the microcomputer. This will, in turn, provide a more complete picture of how this technology mediates the cultural transmission process, as well as a basis for discussing how the professional judgments of the teacher in the instructional uses of the microcomputer relate to the larger question of political empowerment and cultural reform.

CHAPTER 3

Educational Computing: The Selection and Amplification of Culture

The educational ideal of some computer-education experts is exemplified in an educational experiment funded by Apple Computers that is taking place in six sites across the country, including one in Eugene, Oregon. The program is called the Apple Classroom of Tomorrow (ACOT); the site in Eugene involves two middle-school classes of students in what is referred to as a "computer-saturated" curriculum. After taking their first class in the regular part of the school, the students enter a room where every desk is equipped with an Apple IIe computer and every third desk has an ImageWriter printer. There, from 10:00 A.M. until 2:15 P.M., the students interact with software that "delivers" the curriculum: *Math Shop*, LOGO, *Writing Adventure*, *Appleworks*, *Mouse Paint*. This typical exposure may be altered to include *Mastering Fractions*, *Oh, Deer!* (the group simulation game dealing with environmental management discussed in Chapter 2), as well as the use of the computer to teach science and spelling. In effect, all aspects of the curriculum involve the use of the microcomputer; even the scoring of student performance is part of the new technological culture of the classroom. Guided by a teacher who sets a characteristically fast pace ("Hurry up, let's go!"), the students in the Eugene classroom appear actively and enthusiastically engaged (Cooper, 1986). The success, as perceived by local educators and the officials of Apple Computers, confirmed the need to move ahead with a proposal to expand the experiment into an entire middle school of 150 students, ironically to be called the da Vinci Middle School.

This experiment is important to our discussion because it draws attention to a set of issues that need to be addressed by teachers and educational policy makers who are considering the educational uses of this new technology. Educational researchers are already sifting through the test-score data to assess the educational consequences of the computer-saturated classroom. Their findings will be important to consider, but since they tend to view the classroom through a set of conceptual lenses that put in focus only the limited form of learning associated with the ability to represent the newly acquired knowledge to others (generally in the form of information, facts, and judgments that fit the true-false and fill-in formats of educational testing), we shall identify the other forms of learning that are mediated by the use of the microcomputer. That these other forms of learning do not lend themselves to mainstream educational-research procedures does not make them any less important to consider.

For some time now efforts have been made to understand the interactional characteristics of the classroom—the ongoing ecology of verbal and nonverbal communication that makes the classroom so difficult to bring under total technological control (Cazden, Johns, & Hymes, 1972). However, discussions about how to use the microcomputer in the classroom tend to ignore the deeper implications of viewing the classroom as a language ecology. Ironically, in the technologically advanced classrooms the older view of the student as a seemingly self-directing being who is part of the sender-receiver message systems of the classroom still prevails. These message systems are viewed as involving teacher and student (often two-way), textbooks and student (one-way, with student as receiver of information), and student and instructional software program (two-way, depending on nature of the software program). The student-to-student message system is also present but is often seen as outside the teacher's domain of control, and thus as a potential source of disruption. In effect, the use of the microcomputer in the classroom has been grafted onto a traditional set of assumptions about the nature of the individual and the rational process and about the conduit function that, as we saw in the last chapter, has erroneously been attributed to language.

If we start with a different perspective on the classroom, one that takes seriously the processes of cultural transmission and renewal, the effect that the microcomputer has on the educational process will be viewed differently. Unlike the ACOT classroom, where the teacher is continually tabulating test scores and performance data on a record-keeping data disk, we can address a distinctly different set of questions relating to how the use of the microcomputer influences the cultural ecology of the classroom. These questions also apply to the less "computer saturated" classrooms. To put the central question in its most general sense: How does the use of the microcomputer (for purposes of simulation, data base, drill and practice, and so forth) mediate the student's experience of culture? Which aspects of the cultural ecology of the classroom are selected for amplification, and which aspects are reduced?

A starting point for identifying the characteristics of the classroom, ignored by the computer-education experts with their technicist mind-set, is to understand the nature of culture, which constitutes the milieu of the classroom. Again, Clifford Geertz provides a useful explanation: culture "denotes an historically transmitted pattern of meanings embodied in symbols, a system of inherited conceptions expressed in symbolic forms by means of which men communicate, perpetuate, and develop their knowledge about and attitudes toward life" (1973, p. 89). Ward Goodenough suggests that culture can be understood in terms of providing "standards for deciding what can be, standards for deciding how one feels about it, standards for deciding what to do about it, and standards for deciding how to go about doing it" (1981, p. 62). These definitions, though not exhaustive, remove from center stage the autonomous and rational individual who is further empowered by the acquisition of data.

While the Geertz/Goodenough view of culture recognizes that the individual thinks, has feelings and a self-concept, faces moral dilemmas, and so forth, it emphasizes the "patterns" and "standards" that are transmitted from the past through the various language processes that guide the individual's activities. These templates represent the tacit knowledge acquired by the child as the verbal and nonverbal language systems are learned. As Goodenough summarizes it, "To learn the language—that is, to learn to use its vocabulary acceptably—is indispensable for learning the cultural forms its vocabulary encodes" (1981, p. 66). As an example of this we can go back to the process of framing we must enact in mutually recognizable patterns if successful communication is to occur. The use of body language, tone of voice, and so forth must adhere to a shared pattern that signals, for example, that the exchange is at the impersonal, informational level and that personal feelings are to be excluded. The use of a different frame will communicate a meta-message that was not intended. The patterns for social space, organizing time, structuring our thoughts, regulating our emotions, and so forth are also acquired and sustained through communication, but this knowledge is seldom understood at an explicit level of awareness. It is, instead, part of our natural attitude, and as Edward Hall (1977) points out, it is primarily when someone deviates from the taken-for-granted patterns that we become aware of there being a guiding pattern.

This view of culture, when related specifically to the classroom, forces a reappraisal of what is going on there. For example, students should no longer be seen simply as inner directed by their *own* feelings and *own* thought process but rather as largely re-enacting (with minor variations) the tacitly shared patterns—of dress, body language, syntax, thought, and so forth. Similarly, the teacher's rational control of the classroom should also be seen as equally embedded in the deep patterns (including the epistemic categories used to privilege certain forms of knowledge) that constitute the living traditions we know as culture. By recognizing the symbolic foundations for the patterns that guide thought, feelings, and behavior, as well as how these patterns are shared, sustained, and modified through communication, this more culturally oriented view of the classroom helps us see it as an ecology of relationships. These relationships, which make the classroom such a dynamic environment, are regulated largely by the patterns (information codes handed down from the past) the participants have internalized as part of their taken-for-granted view of the world.

One of the most important implications of this view, which was more fully articulated by Gregory Bateson, is that the individual is seen as part of a larger information-sharing network. But the knowledge that guides the process of interacting with others is not seen as exclusively located in the mind of the individual. In *Steps to an Ecology of Mind* (1974) Bateson states that "the total self-corrective unit which processes information, or, as I say, 'thinks' and 'acts' and 'decides,' is a *system* whose boundaries do not at all coincide with the boundaries of the body or of what is popularly called the 'self' or 'consciousness.'" The system or network includes all the "pathways along which information can travel" (p. 319). These networks of information exchange are the basis of making the adjustments necessary for the survival of the ecology of relationships that constitute the system. To relate this aspect of Bateson's thinking to the classroom, the student, the objects in the classroom like desks and computers, the other students and teacher, the layout of space, and so forth can be viewed as part of an informational ecology. Interaction occurs by taking account of the information communicated through the interacting parts that make up the field of relationships. Differences within this field lead to information exchanges that, in turn, modify the patterns of subsequent interaction. The following example was used by Bateson to explain the idea that the "mental process is always a sequence of interactions *between* parts":

> Consider a man felling a tree with an axe. Each stroke of the axe is modified or corrected, according to the shape of the cut face of the tree left by the previous stroke. This self-corrective (i.e., mental) process is brought about by a total system, tree–eyes–brain–muscles–axe-stroke–tree; and it is this total system that has the characteristics of immanent mind. More correctly, we could spell out the matter as: (differences in tree)–(differences in retina)–(differences in brain)–(differences in muscles)–(differences in movement of axe)–(differences in tree), etc. What is transmitted around the circuit is transforms of differences. And, as noted above, the differences which make the difference is an *idea* or unit of information. (1974, pp. 317–18)

In relating Bateson's view to the classroom, we can see that the student–chair–print or video screen–keyboard–teacher (including body language and verbal communication)–time of the clock–other students–previously announced assignment–and so forth are all part of an information exchange. But unlike the example of the individual who adjusts the dynamics of cutting down the tree by participating in a circuit of information, the information exchange that characterizes the context in which the student is situated involves, in addition to adjustments based on new information exchanged between the interacting parts, utilizing preexisting cultural patterns as a guide for action. In effect, the individual's involvement is mediated by culture. Much of the communication that makes up the ecology of the ongoing information exchanges in the classroom involves communicating these patterns (including the individual's interpretation of them) as guides for acting in socially predictable (and acceptable) ways.

For example, in the student–teacher–lesson–time-left-in-the-period information exchange, the teacher's behavioral patterns help to frame what will be perceived as the appropriate behavioral patterns for students; for example, maintaining eye contact with the teacher or at least exhibiting the body language that signals they are part of the teacher-directed information exchange rather than a new one that is being started up by a student sitting four seats from the back. The shared awareness that the class period is almost over (also part of the information exchange that changes the ongoing dynamics) may lead to a reframing process wherein the teacher (now signaling a more relaxed demeanor by sitting on the desk) and students interact in accordance with the behaviors dictated by a new set of patterns (i.e., more casual and personal conversation interspersed with friendly joking) that would have been totally inappropriate to the previously more formal phase of the class period.

Understanding classroom interaction as information exchanges that involve introducing students to new patterns (information codes) that are to be used as guides in new social situations as well as reinforcing previously learned patterns brings us back to our original question: How does the use of the microcomputer, as part of an ecology of relationships, influence the student's experience of culture? Stated somewhat differently, which aspects of the shared information codes that constitute the language community's view of reality are selected by computer technology for amplification, and which are reduced (or entirely eliminated) in the cultural transmission process? In a sense we are returning to the question of whether the computer is a neutral technology, but we are approaching it from the angle of the ecology of relationships and codes we know as culture. This is important for understanding how the educational use of the microcomputer influences our own conceptual templates and thus our ability to address the problems we face as a society, as well as the influence this technology will have on non-Western cultures.

LANGUAGE AND DIGITAL THINKING

Language is an important starting point, since it provides, as Schon points out, the interpretative (generative metaphors) framework for understanding what is being communicated in the informational networks that constitute society and our relationships with the natural environment. Language both influences what we are able to think about and enables us to communicate our thoughts to others. In this sense it facilitates and binds at the same time (Pitkin, 1973). An example is the way in which computer-education experts' unconscious dependence on generative metaphors that represent technology as a tool, language as a conduit, and rational thought as a basis of efficacious control shapes their discourse in a manner that ignores most of the issues we have dealt with. This is an example of how language *largely* sets the boundaries of what we are able to think about and, at the same time, frames our way of understanding. Although language should not be viewed as entirely controlling thought, its power to influence thought (witness our recent discovery of how our language patterns have maintained gender distinctions in our social relationships) can be viewed as a regulator of our political experience. To reiterate Claus Mueller's insight, not only is language a conceptual guidance system, it is a political one as well (1973).

As students interact with the microcomputer, they are involved in a process of communication (an information exchange in Bateson's sense of the phrase) that is very much influenced by the cultural assumptions and epistemic categories embedded in the language-thought processes of the person who wrote the software program. It is a relationship analogous to that of the reader and the author of a text. There is, however, a tradition of asking questions about the conceptual biases of a book's author; the emphasis on information processing and the complexity of using the technology have made it more difficult to recognize the human authorship of the programs. Moreover, because the metaphors of data and information suggest objectivity in their conceptual framing, it seems perfectly natural to refer to "collecting data" but unnatural to refer to "constructing data." The language that presents the data on the screen or is typed by the student as a response to the commands of the program provides the conceptual foothold for thinking. Thus the way in which the microcomputer mediates (amplifies or reduces) the student's experience of culture, by the way of the printed work, can be seen in whether the software program makes available a limited language code or a more complex and metaphorically rich one. Thus the use of microcomputers, when used as the chief medium for learning about a new subject, cannot be separated from the question of language socialization.

As suggested earlier, language socialization is also political socialization. As demonstrated in the language used to transmit information about the experience of the pioneers on the Oregon Trail, the students' understanding is framed in a manner that prevents them from viewing the message exchanges (which are a way of viewing the attacks on the pioneers) from the perspective of the indigenous peoples. This example helps to demonstrate how the control of language can influence students' ability to recognize certain forms of information that emerge from the relationships being studied.

But there is another way in which the microcomputer can be understood as amplifying certain characteristics of culture and reducing others. The justification widely used by the advocates of educational computing that students must be computer literate in order to participate fully in the information-based society of the future sounds on the surface to be highly reasonable. But that is exactly the problem: it is a surface way of thinking about the forms of knowledge that have authority in our lives. Indeed, we do collect and process a great deal of information. But being able to manipulate information, even with the speed and accuracy of a computer, is not the same as thinking. This is the vitally important point that is missed by educators who urge the adoption of the new technology on the grounds that we are moving into the Information Age.

Theodore Roszak is also interested in people's being able to lead intelligent and productive lives in the future, but he warns us of the danger of confusing information with ideas. While agreeing that computers greatly extend our ability to process information, Roszak nevertheless argues that the data merchants, futurologists, and those who believe that computer literacy is the only appropriate educational path to the future have "lost sight of the paramount truth that the *mind thinks with ideas, not with information*" (1986, p. 88). Since Roszak's point is critically important to understanding the amplification and reduction characteristics of educational computing, it is important to follow his thinking about this critical distinction, particularly when the statement that we do not think with information must sound so outlandish to the advocates of computer literacy:

> Information may helpfully illustrate or decorate an idea; it may, where it works under the guidance of a contrasting idea, help to call other ideas into question. But information does not create ideas; by itself, it does not validate or invalidate them. An idea can only be generated, revised, or unseated by another idea. A culture survives by the power, plasticity, and fertility of its ideas. Ideas come first, because ideas define, contain, and eventually produce information. The principal task of education, therefore, is to teach young minds how to deal with ideas: how to evaluate them, extend them, adapt them to new uses. This can be done with the use of very little information, perhaps none at all. It certainly does not require data processing machinery of any kind. An excess of information may actually crowd out ideas, leaving the mind (young minds especially) distracted by sterile, disconnected facts, lost among shapeless heaps of data. (1986, p. 88)

Roszak's warning about the danger of too much information crowding out ideas was borne out in an exchange in a Florida high school between a teacher and a student who had completed an assignment by turning in a massive computer printout. "Frank," the teacher said, "stop a moment. I think it's great that you have gathered all these facts about the subject, but put them aside for just a second. Look at me and tell me in your own words: What do you *feel about this issue*?" After staring blankly for a moment, Frank replied, "I don't know what you mean" (quoted in Berman, 1986, p. 35). The problem here reflects a basic confusion about what is involved in the process of thinking. Frank had simply assumed that gathering and processing information involves thinking—a view that is reinforced in the educational-computing literature. Where Papert stands on this issue will be addressed later.

Thinking, according to Roszak, is organized by what he terms "master ideas"—or what Schon refers to as "generative metaphors." Others have used such terms as *paradigm* and *worldview* to describe the basic templates that give individual experience, social norms and institutions, and a people's moral and conceptual practices a sense of coherence and legitimacy. The Christian idea of original sin, the Enlightenment idea that rational thought is the source of empowerment, and the current idea that data is the basis of our intellectual authority are three examples of master ideas. At the surface level of our symbolic world we are continually creating new master ideas (often but not necessarily derived from the ideas that are at the core of the cultural belief system) that guide how we conceptualize a problem and understand relationships. As an example, the idea of computer literacy is based on a master idea that equates thinking with information processing. As we go deeper into the archeology of this generative metaphor we find the master idea that represents the person in the image of the machine. We also encounter a language that continues to frame our way of thinking in accordance with this master idea—measurement, experiment, technique, (and now) data-based decision making, feedback, interface, and so forth.

Roszak (1986) makes two further points that are essential to consider. The first is that the master ideas that influence what we will perceive as relevant information are experienced at a subliminal or taken-for-granted level. The data we gather through the measurement of time, for example, are based on a highly complex master idea that goes back to the foundations of our Judeo-Christian heritage and is now so commonplace that it has become part of our natural attitude toward everyday life. Few people are aware of the assumptions that underlie our view of time or understand the historical forces that shaped it into its present form. Roszak's second point is that the master ideas are not derived from data or information, but from insight, conviction, and imagination that is attuned to the need to understand and improve the human situation. Some master ideas, viewed from a twisted vantage point, have fostered inequality and violence, while others have provided the conceptual and moral basis for genuine advancement of the human condition. Regardless of how we now view the content of these master ideas, they represent an aspect of human thought that is vitally important to our consideration of the educational effects of the microcomputer—namely, the metaphorical nature of thought. When we take the time to uncover the origin of such guiding master ideas—be they positive or negative—as original sin, racial superiority, human equality, nonviolent political action as a basis of social reform, world peace, ecological balance, and so forth, we find an archetypal story that is used to explain how the human situation should be understood and to provide guidance for future behavior. Master ideas are, in effect, derived from the metaphorical nature of our thought process. Even the less deeply embedded master ideas that guide our thinking about research and policy decisions are derived from an analogic starting point—that is, an interpretation of some aspect of past human experience that is used as a reference point for understanding the new and unfamiliar.

By recasting Roszak's distinction between ideas and information in terms of metaphorical (analogic) and digital thinking, we come back to the problem of computer literacy in the Information Age. When learning is mediated by the microcomputer, the digital form of thinking is amplified. This is illustrated in the following explanation of how the program called BOGBOD, written in micro-Prolog, supposedly leads students to simulate the thought process of the historian:

> The computer's role in detective exercises like BOGBOD is to provide a data base containing historical information which is structured so that pupils can have meaningful access to it. This structuring enables pupils to establish a logical pattern of question, answer, assimilation and new questioning. The pupils thus *acquire a series of mental building blocks from their interaction with the computer. The students can use these building blocks to construct logical structures in their minds*. (Nichol and Dean, 1984, p. 192; italics added)

Similarly, Papert's LOGO is based on the assumption that, as he puts it, "when knowledge can be broken up into 'mind-size bites,' it is more communicable, more assimilable, more simply constructable. . . . Learning consists of building up a set of materials and tools that one can handle and manipulate" (1980, p. 171). To use Roszak's phrase, Papert and the designers of BOGBOD have given us an "information processing model" of the mind; it is, in effect, a view of digital thinking wherein following *procedure* becomes essential to organizing discrete and decontextualized bits of information into the building blocks upon which thought is to be based.

Although in the previous chapter we have already discussed the metaphorical nature of language and thought, it is essential that we clarify the difference between metaphorical (analogic being one type) and digital thinking. This will enable us to put in perspective the larger implication of not recognizing that while the microcomputer may be highly suited to storing, manipulating, and retrieving information, it is a poorly suited technology for providing the basis of metaphorical thinking and for communicating the analogue knowledge of a culture. It will also help clarify why it is fundamentally wrong, in an educational, political, and moral sense, to equate machine "intelligence" with human intelligence.

In the most basic sense digital thinking involves conscious intent in manipulating bits of information. It can deal only with what has been abstracted from context and made explicit, like the date of an event, the parts of the body or a machine, the events of a historical period (names, places, actions, and so forth). Digital knowledge, in effect, involves separating the parts from the whole, like letters in a word or the words that make up a sentence, and then reconstituting the parts through a linear form of thinking. In abstracting these parts, such as information made available in a newspaper story or data base, one loses sight of the context of relationships—that is, the whole.

McClintock's explanation of how culture, this "vast store of externalized memory" as he put it, is being converted over to binary code summarizes how the characteristics of computer technology help constitute a digital form of knowledge. In "Marking the Second Frontier," he writes:

> Digital technologies do not transmit one thing that is analogous to another, the real matter in question. Rather, a digital technology transmits exact, or nearly exact, values, as precisely as these can be represented in binary code. . . . The key to digital technology, compared to analog, is the digital absence of ambiguity: it deals with successive states, either-or conditions in which a circuit is either off or it is on. . . . Insofar as something can be described accurately in binary code, it can be *recreated* from that code. (1988, p. 347)

As emphasized in McClintock's statement, the tacit dimensions of experience, which are a source of meaning, understanding, and pattern, are to be ignored as too ambiguous to be accurately represented. Digital knowledge provides information that is taken out of context and then situated in a new and often highly abstract one that is constructed through the interpretative efforts of the person who is attempting to make sense of data or information. In effect, the use of digital knowledge involves the falsification of the context, but ironically this is seen by others, such as Papert and the advocates of BOGBOD, as an irrelevant concern, since they view individuals as using data to create their own building blocks. Digital thinking, in a sense, is attractive partly because it reinforces the cultural assumption that we are autonomous individuals who can rationally construct the world we want. But there is a real cost when this analytical, linear form of thinking becomes the dominant form rather than a complement to a more broadly based form of metaphorical thinking.

Recognizing the importance of analogue knowledge (the outcome of a more self-conscious process of metaphorical thinking) involves going against the grain of currently held myths about the nature of individual agency, the progressive nature of technological change, and the culture-free nature of the rational process. But our historical dependence upon analogue knowledge has been a vitally important aspect of human experience, even though it is being eclipsed by the digital knowledge that fuels scientific and technological advances—which, incidentally, have largely ignored the importance of context (i.e., both the cultural and natural ecology).

Unlike digital thinking, which is linear, componential, and abstracting, analogic thinking involves relationships, context, redundancy, and memory. It also involves a tacit level of pattern recognition, such as how to form into a line when purchasing a ticket, how to tell a story in three parts, and how to know that another person's body language is to be interpreted as a friendly greeting. Analogue knowledge serves as a guide to understanding the present and thus involves a continuity between the past and the present. The patterns, as information codes learned in the past, are redundant in the sense that we recognize their reproduction in the present and thus have a basis for determining how to proceed. Without redundancy (a word that carries a negative connotation for people whose thinking is shaped by the generative metaphor of autonomous individual), the new situation would have to be understood entirely on its own terms, which would be an impossibility for both linguistic and cognitive reasons. Although I do not agree entirely with the distinction that Bateson makes between digital and analogue knowledge, I would like to use his explanation of the role of redundancy in analogic thinking:

> "Meaning" may be regarded as an approximate synonym of pattern, redundancy, information, and "restraint," within a paradigm of the following sort: Any aggregate of events or objects (e.g., a sequence of phonemes, a painting, or a frog, or a culture) shall be said to contain "redundancy" or "pattern" if the aggregate can be divided in any way by a "slash mark," such that an observer perceiving only what is on one side of the slash mark can *guess*, with better than random success, what is on the other side of the slash mark. We may say that what is on one side of the slash mark contains *information* or has *meaning* about what is on the other side. Or, in the engineer's language, the aggregate contains "redundancy." (Bateson, 1974, p. 131)

In the ongoing ecology of relationships we continually encounter only part of a message exchange—the averting of eye contact within a certain social context, a tone of voice that has a certain edge to it, the turning of a corner—and we have to guess across the slash mark in order to fill in what is missing. In these situations, which characterize most of our daily activities, the present is understood because it has elements that are like the patterns we have learned in the past. The dependency and tacit nature of our analogue knowledge was brought home to me when I encountered the checkout clerk in the English equivalent of our supermarket. After placing the basket of groceries on the counter I mentally crossed over the slash mark (i.e., a guess—really an expectation borne of past experience—about the behavioral pattern that would then be exhibited by the clerk) by re-enacting the behavioral pattern we all take for granted as Americans. But this time the tacit knowledge that governs the clerk-customer relationship back home did not work. After paying for the goods, which involved the usual complex exchange of messages at the paralinguistic level, I found myself looking at all the groceries still piled up at the end of the counter. While I waited for the clerk to bag them, the other people standing in line began to communicate at a nonverbal level a sense of annoyance and impatience. Then the insight came that this situation was not entirely analogous to the patterns I was accustomed to; here the expectation was that I was to bag my own groceries.

This example of guessing across the slash marks of what is given in a social exchange by using analogue knowledge as a guide is reenacted continually by all of us every day. What this admittedly trivial example brings out is the pervasiveness of our dependence on analogic thinking: in preparing a meal, greeting another person, viewing our relationship to the environment, and making sense of our daily achievements. It also suggests something about the taken-for-granted nature of this form of thinking—including our tendency to not recognize redundancy as a necessary element that enables us to give meaning to the present by connecting it to the past. Or, to put it another way, memory of past pattern-context-message exchanges is essential to a life of coherence, meaning, connectedness, and predictability.

There is another aspect of metaphorical thinking that is important to acknowledge as we as a society, in our general ignorance of how science and technology have been used as the generative metaphor for a new epistemology, increasingly confer importance on digital thinking. This has to do with the connection between metaphorical thinking and our sense of morality—that is, our sense of responsibility toward the other. The novelist Cynthia Ozick makes an important observation about the ancient Greeks' treatment of strangers as despised barbarians that relates directly to Bateson's insights into the nature and importance of metaphorical thinking. The Greeks, she writes,

> never undertook to imagine what it was to be the Other; the outsider; the alien; the slave; the oppressed; the sufferer; the outcast; the opponent; the barbarian who owns feeling and deserves rights. And that is because they did not, as a society, cultivate memory, or search out any historical metaphor to contain memory. (1986, p. 66)

Imagining what it is like "to be the Other" is the same as taking seriously, in terms of the memories of one's own eventful experiences, what is on the other side of the slash marks; that is, understanding the Other as being like oneself—having the desire for dignity, a meaningful life, and being taken seriously by others.

In explaining how moral sensitivity to the Other is grounded in metaphorical thinking, Ozick stresses that metaphor is the opposite of inspiration and abstraction. Neither one takes account of how the pattern of an experience suffered over generations becomes in the collective memory of a people the basis of a metaphor serving to concentrate insight and the resolve to base future experience on a new moral principal. As an example of how memory is converted into a metaphor, she reminds us that "four hundred years of bondage in Egypt, rendered as metaphoric memory, can be spoken in a moment; in a single sentence. . . . 'Love thy neighbor as thyself'" (1986, p. 67). For examples of the institutionalization of metaphoric memory, and thus of what is supposed to constitute the moral patterns that will avoid the perils of the past, we can point to the Constitutional guarantees of freedom of speech, a public school system that fosters universal literacy, and laws that protect equality of opportunity. The experience of the past is retained as part of the community of memory embedded in the metaphorical nature of our language, thus providing the analogues for a morally defensible life. Memory, in effect, is the basis necessary for a critical interpretation of the present; and in being the thread that connects the events of our life together into a coherent whole, it also serves to constitute the image of self as a metaphor. But not all the experiences of the past provide ecologically or morally defensible analogues for basing present experience—a point that may be lost sight of by the compelling nature of Ozick's example. Analogues are basic to the human thought process, but they require a critical interpretation—which means being able to place them in their historical and cultural context.

The digital computer, programmed with a language code that directs the logical functions that can be performed on inputs, is a marvelous machine. Indeed, the student who moves from book to microcomputer must experience a genuine sense of awe at the versatility of this new technology. But since our concern is with education rather than the promotion of a particular technology, it is important to ask about the consequences of having educational decisions made by the classroom teacher, the person who writes the instructional software program, and the educational-computer experts when they do not, for the most part, know the difference between analogic and digital thinking. And in not understanding this difference, they will be unable to make intelligent judgments about the deeper implications of the educational technology they choose. Since we shall return in the next chapter to the professional judgments surrounding the educational uses of microcomputers, we will conclude this section by identifying some of the dangers associated with reducing the educational process to the acquisition and manipulation of information. The warnings apply not only to the information-processing model of thinking associated with educational computing but also to textbooks, with their inert facts and more primitive, noninteractive language code.

What is most likely to catch the public eye about our tendency to promote the educational use of technologies that amplify digital thinking is the observation by the director of the Sony Research Center, Makoto Kikuchi (1981), that the Japanese culture reinforces a mode of thinking that does not have the linear, componential, and logical (digital) characteristics of our orientation but instead relies upon understanding through pattern recognition. By way of contrast, we are comfortable in thinking in terms of "yes-no," and "when this happens, do this," and data-based decision making, which is procedural in nature. A partial explanation for the Japanese being more analogic thinkers, while we are more digital, might be found in the conceptual differences fostered by the use of the Roman-style alphabet (digital) and the use of Chinese characters (analogic) (Ramsey, 1984). The important point for us is that the causes of our digital orientation are deeply rooted in our cultural past. Computers are both a result of this "yes-no" logical pattern and, now, a powerful source of reinforcement.

To avoid getting our line of analysis confused with the current educational debate fostered by the affront to our national ego caused by the superiority of a non-Western technological power, I want to touch briefly on why the educational technologies that foster digital thinking must be balanced by approaches to passing on those aspects of culture that strengthen the foundations of analogic thinking. We are not just a digital culture, even though to the outsider it might seem that we are both obsessive and exceedingly naive about basing ideas on the authority of "objective" information. As Bateson (1974) notes, our everyday experiences are largely guided by the redundancy factor in pattern recognition. This fund of analogue knowledge is learned in context and primarily at the tacit level. This form of knowledge is unconsciously reinforced in schools (e.g., signaling intent to get involved by raising one's hand, using dress as an information code to communicate group membership, and so forth), even as students are learning new information. The aspect of analogue knowledge that schools need to deal with in a more systematic manner can be more clearly illustrated with a metaphor that is being increasingly used to recover a deeper sense of who we are—namely, that what is distinctive about being human is that we are storytellers and, thus, participants in a "community of memory" (Bellah, Madsen, Sullivan, Swidler, and Tipton, 1985, p. 153). This is quite different from the liberal view of the autonomous individual, which surely must be viewed as an outgrowth of the male-dominated intellectual heritage that has emphasized the digital over the analogic. Alasdair MacIntyre has given us a particularly good explanation of humankind as storyteller:

> What the narrative concept of selfhood requires is thus twofold. On the one hand, I am what I may justifiably be taken by others to be in the course of living out a story that runs from my birth to my death; I am the *subject* of a history that is my own and no one else's, that has its own peculiar meaning. When someone complains—as do some of those who attempt to commit suicide—that his or her life is meaningless, he or she is often and perhaps characteristically complaining that the narrative of their life has become unintelligible to them, that it lacks any point, any movement towards a climax or a *telos*. Hence the point of doing any one thing rather than another at crucial junctures in their lives seems to such person to have been lost. . . . The other aspect of narrative selfhood is correlative: I am not only accountable, I am one who can always ask others for an account, who can put others to the question. I am part of their story, as they are part of mine. The narrative of any one life is part of an interlocking set of narratives. Moreover this asking for and giving of accounts itself plays an important part in constituting narratives. . . . In what does the unity of an individual life consist? The answer is that its

unity is the unity of a narrative embodied in a single life. (1984, pp. 217–18)

The educational implications of his statement are twofold, and both suggest an approach to transmitting analogue knowledge that does not fit the digital amplifying characteristics of educational computing—even when used in the format of a simulation program. The first implication involves learning about the master ideas, or root metaphors, that have served as the storyline of a cultural group, period, or event (e.g., the French or American revolution). But they need to be understood as giving form to the culture (its art, ways of knowing, social institutions, economic practices, technological development, spiritual development, and so forth), as well as being reformed over time by the internal and external cultural forces at work. Recognizing the patterns re-enacted in an individual life in relationship to the shared patterns of the cultural group provides a way of thinking that may strengthen students' ability to see their own lives as more than a series of disconnected events. But learning at a subliminal as well as explicit level the models or patterns that have been the basis of other lives is only a prerequisite for being able to think relationally.

As Bellah and his co-authors suggest, students must also be able to hold others as well as themselves to account—that is, to question and think critically from a perspective that is grounded in an understanding of a community of metaphoric memory about good and evil: "stories of shared suffering," "suffering inflicted," "of what a good character is like," and "the future as a community of hope" (1985, p. 153). Without models or analogues of how to deal with the ever-changing moments in an individual's existential situation, the development of the power of critical reflection may foster the sense that everything is relative and, thus, that only the immediate needs of the individual matter.

The conceptual foundations of analogic thinking and moral behavior require a different emphasis than that given to us by the advocates of educational computing. The starting point should not be data and simulation as the basis of thinking but rather how to think with and about ideas, where they came from, how they provide the conceptual templates that guide our technical activities and moral relationships, how our natural language influences our way of knowing, and how the language-thought connection is rooted in metaphorical imagination—all of which makes intelligence, in part, an unconscious form of recollection. But this shift in emphasis, which they may see as the betrayal of youth needing to become computer literate and thus citizens of the Information Age, requires an awareness that the microcomputer is culturally selective in what it can be used to transmit. Besides recognizing how educational software programs weaken the forms of knowledge associated with metaphorical thinking, we must also understand how the technology selects out for amplification and reduction other aspects of the culture. We shall now turn to how tradition, individualism, and orality are represented to students through this technology.

THE TECHNOCRATIC VIEW OF TIME

In his influential book, *Mindstorms*, Seymour Papert makes the observation that "the computer is not a culture in itself, but it can serve to advance very different cultural and philosophical outlooks" (1980, p. 31). Papert's purpose in making this statement was to emphasize that while he recognized LOGO could be used within the traditional classroom, with its formal curriculum, he saw its real educational benefits occurring in a classroom where students could "build their own intellectual structures with materials drawn from the surrounding culture" (pp. 31–32). Later we shall take a critical look at the myth of individualism that underlies the ideology of mainstream educational computing; for now we shall modify Papert's insight, in order to avoid the interpretation that technology is neutral, by expanding on its implications in ways that perhaps Papert himself did not fully understand. The specific aspect of a cultural and philosophical (ideological) outlook promoted through educational computing we shall now examine relates to the sense of time that is amplified through this technology. In the ensuing discussion we must keep in mind that we are really dealing with the cultural assumptions of the people who create the technology—the machine languages and instructional software programs. However, this qualification should not be interpreted as meaning that if people held different cultural assumptions they could, through new programming techniques, use the computer to represent a different view of our relationship to time.

People working on the leading edge of computer technology appear to share the facile optimism expressed by Pamela McCorduck, an ideologue of the fifth-generation of computers, that "these machines will automatically pave and shape . . . large quantities of information into the knowledge we want, so that our limited human brains can comprehend and make use of it" (1985, p. 39). Each new advance in the technology, like the work now being done on parallel processing, is accepted as a sign of progress and further evidence that computers are the technology of this century. Experts on the educational uses of computers also share this optimism and see in Joseph Weizenbaum's reservations little to take seriously. The title of Tom Snyder and Jane Palmer's book, *In Search of the Most Amazing Thing* (1986), suggests the ambience of this group. What interests us here is not the unqualified optimism that characterizes the computer experts who see themselves as leading us into the promised land of power, prediction, and control—the secular vision of the technocrats, who also heralded the introduction of nuclear technology—but the less spectacular problem of how their cultural assumptions about the nature of time, and our place in it, are amplified through the use of microcomputers in the classroom.

Computer amplification of a cultural outlook on how to view ourselves in time (i.e., our orientation toward past, present, and future) can be seen in the emphasis that is placed on information storage and retrieval. The following statement by McClintock, part of which was cited earlier, captures the view of the individual's relationship to time that characterizes the field of educational computing: "Culture, as it has accumulated in history, is a vast store of externalized memory, memories that are put into things outside of human brains, into things that endure, inert but stable" (1988, p. 350). According to this view, the individual stands apart from the past as a rational, self-directing agent. The relationship is essentially that of a spectator who may choose to validate some aspect of past by remembering it. As McClintock puts it, we relate to past culture "exclusively in the remembrance of things" (p. 351). The data base thus becomes the repository of factual information that can be used instrumentally for solving a current problem. If the individual does not see the past as having instrumental value or cannot remember it, then, according to this view, the past is disconnected from the present. The linkage of the past to the present is established on a permanent basis when some aspect of the past—books, songs, chronologies of events, and so forth—is represented in binary code and stored in a data base.

Although the view of the culture and tradition (the temporal aspect of culture) associated with Geertz and Goodenough more accurately represents how students unconsciously re-enact the conceptual, social, and psychological patterns shared by their language community, the educational use of the microcomputer reinforces the more Cartesian view of the individual as the detached observer who is empowered through the acquisition of objective knowledge (Bordo, 1987; Rorty, 1979). This Cartesian view of knowledge is based on a mind-body dualism that not only established the primacy of procedural thinking and a mechanistic view of the external world but also a sense of detachment from the rhythms of culture and nature. The Cartesian emphasis on the explicit nature of knowledge was essential for establishing the objective and distancing nature of thought (the "mirror of nature" to use Rorty's phrase). This, in turn, allowed for a view of the individual who is not embedded in the continuities that connect the present to the past.

The arguments for educational computing in all its possibilities, as well as the development of expert systems and other computer applications, all appear to represent the individual as disconnected from the past. As stated in a current textbook, *Computer Strategies for Education*, "the most important characteristic of effective problem solvers is their ability to acquire new conceptual tools" (Kinzer, Sherwood, and Bransford, 1986, p. 187). The same temporal sense of individual autonomy is expressed in the statement by Joel S. Birnbaum of Hewlett-Packard Laboratories: "Intelligent data agents will provide a greatly enhanced ability to search global data bases to find desired information without providing such detailed parameters for the search. . . . [and] expert-systems technology allows us to synthesize diffuse human wisdom unlikely to be found in a single individual, and to reuse it across different domains" (1985, p. 137). Although Birnbaum's view of expert systems, wherein individuals can acquire the information that supposedly underlies the judgment of the physician, lawyer, potter, and so forth, fails to take account of the complex interrelationship of context—experiences that involve both the tacit and explicit forms of understanding that Michael Oakeshott (1962) is concerned about—it is representative of how the computer is seen as a means of empowering individuals who are supposedly disconnected from the past.

This view, which is neatly summarized in Papert's statement that individuals "build *their own* intellectual structures" (1980, p. 32), is part of the socialization process that influences how students learn how to think of themselves in relation to the past. And like other socially constructed views of reality that are difficult to question because of their taken-for-granted nature (e.g., the sexist attitudes that were learned at the commonsense level), it is basically incorrect. Not only does this view reflect the Cartesian bias against the recognition of nonpropositional forms of knowledge (i.e., the cultural analogues that are a common aspect of everyday experience); it is based on a basic misunderstanding of how traditions, with roots deep in the past, are re-enacted by individuals as they think and communicate with others, use technologies, depend upon the predictability of institutional arrangements, and so forth. The structure of our language, and the reality it helps to construct, is not something that individuals create for themselves; nor do they invent the other patterns that govern how they organize and use social space. Our symbol systems, technologies, and institutions are handed down from the past; as Edward Shils observes, while these traditions are indispensable, "they are also seldom entirely adequate" (1981, p. 213). Living traditions are taken for granted and provide the patterns for thought and action; traditions from the past that no longer seem appropriate are often made explicit, revised, and, in many instances, discarded entirely. Shils's point is that regardless of how ideologies (conceptual lenses) condition individuals to view themselves on the continuum of time, traditions of the past are re-enacted in the present—as is occurring here as I use a traditional alphabet, write from left to right, and conform to linguistic and conceptual conventions that go far back in time. Traditions, in a very real sense, provide the authority for our thoughts and actions; it is also important to view them as fluid, continually being modified to fit new circumstances.

The individual's relationship to the past is often obscured because it is embedded in forms of knowledge (tacit and analogue knowledge memory, the epistemic orientation of our language, and so forth) that are not taken seriously by the Cartesian-technicist paradigm, which must be seen as a guiding conceptual tradition that still dominates most areas of educational thought, including educational computing. The emphasis on data and information, the view of language as a conduit for transmitting information between individuals, and the view of individuals as inventing "their own intellectual structures and aids to thinking" (Snyder and Palmer, 1986, p. 98) simply strengthen the conceptual framing that separates the present from its natural continuum with the past, information from its historical and cultural context, and the individual from the discursive formations that, like an inverted pyramid, extend into the unconscious past.

Given this counterview of how individuals are situated in the past-present-future continuum that characterizes their temporality, we must ask the pedagogically significant question: How does the transmission of culture through the educational use of a microcomputer influence students' sense of themselves in relation to the continuum of time? Does the manipulation of a data base or involvement in a simulation exercise contribute to their understanding of the complex relationship between present practices and the traditions of the past, or does it create the sense that they are free of the influence of the past as they make their data-based decisions? The hardcore advocates of educational computing are likely to respond that the massive storage potential of the computer's "memory" enables the teacher and students to collect historical data, thus providing the most useful technology for learning about the past. The problem with this argument is that the information about the past, while useful in certain learning situations, is segmented into facts and data, taken out of context, and generally represented as historically distant from the taken-for-granted traditions that are re-enacted in the student's own experience. Learning about the past in a way that puts out of focus the tacit knowledge that links the past to the student's everyday life simply strengthens the false belief in an individual autonomy wherein the individual judges the past and chooses the future.

Aside from the problem of recognizing the continuities that connect the student's own experience with the past, there is also the educational problem of creating simulation programs that reinforce students for projecting into the past their own taken-for-granted patterns of thinking. An example is a history simulation entitled *Drake*; it is, according to its designers, a "decision-making simulation in which students are encouraged to role-play with a view to gaining an insight into a historical situation and also to establish empathy with the central character" (Adams and Jones, 1983, p. 103). But the decision-making process that students follow as they project themselves into the sixteenth-century, high-seas adventure involves acquiring the fragmentary bits of information essential for understanding the events. The process of role playing, wherein the participants attempt to understand the state of consciousness of that historical period, turns out to be a matter of making decisions about the strategic movement of ships, dealing with dissident crew members, and adjusting local decisions to the risk factors in England's international relations with Spain and Portugal. Simulating Admiral Drake's process of decision making as he faced the contingencies of weather, war, and international politics provides students a useful learning experience pertaining to the factual aspects of Drake's sea saga. But it is miseducational in the sense that the program fails to provide students with an understanding of the historically and culturally different ways of thinking that separate the sixteenth century from the present. In effect, the students are being taught that the pattern of thinking that characterizes their own natural attitude can be projected into the past. This leads to two undesirable consequences. The first is that students are being conditioned to view the past in terms of objective facts and dates, rather than in terms of differences in ways of thinking. The second is that this present-centric view of time, whereby the past is judged in terms of present assumptions and conceptual categories, diminishes the possibility of questioning the foundations of the present mode of consciousness and how it has evolved over time.

This simulation, as well as the others we have looked at, demonstrates that how students are taught to view their relationship to the past depends in part on the program writers' ideology; that is, their understanding—or nonunderstanding—of the role traditions play in creating the tacit knowledge that gives each historical period its distinctive pre-understandings for making sense of experience. Given the modernizing bias that characterizes the departments of computer science and education, where these people are likely to receive their formal training, it is unlikely that they would even be aware of the nature of traditions or the simple but vitally important fact that once traditions are forgotten, or cease to be transmitted, they are permanently lost. That is, lost traditions cannot be recovered as a living part of people's lives, even though they may be restored as dead rituals. In addition to how the ideology of the person who writes the instructional program influences students' ways of thinking about their place in the continuum of time, there is a serious question of whether the inputting of data can be done in a manner that avoids separating it from its context and genealogy—that is, its development as part of a larger cultural configuration of thought and practice that has evolved over time. If the sense of duration (development over time) cannot be part of the input, the microcomputer will amplify the cultural orientation that treats facts and data as nonhistorical.

THE MYTH OF INDIVIDUALISM

Articles and books on educational computing invariably contain references to students that are based on the assumption they are self-directing, autonomous individuals. Through a variety of words and phrases the literature reinforces the dominant metaphor for thinking about the self: "the idea that the knowledge that you have is something you make. . . . The power of LOGO lies in its ability to allow you to do what you want with it" (Papert, quoted in Reinhold, 1986, pp. 35–36); "as BOGBOD is reliant upon *student-initiated* behavior for its learning outcomes, it meets most of Bloom's learning criteria" (Nichol and Dean, 1984, p. 192); and, in a comment about *MacPaint*, "by making it easy for us to create images and work with them, the Macintosh can help us to think" (Benzon, 1985, p. 114). The phrases *you, student-initiated*, and *helps us to think* are variations on the image of self as an individual who has inner feelings, engages in a thought process that is autonomous (except for the inputs of information), and is self-directing in the sense of making his or her own choices.

As Bellah and colleagues explain in *Habits of the Heart* (1985), the idea of individualism has both formed our early national character and itself undergone important mutations in response to perceived limitations in this collectively shared identity. The metaphorical image of the individual as the author of feelings, thoughts, and actions is thus not the creation of the people who write about classroom computing and conceptualize the instructional software. Just as most of the rest of us have been socialized to a discourse that causes us to take for granted a view of knowledge that privileges vision (exemplified in the use of words and phrases such as *insight, perspective, overview, far-sighted, survey, point of view, clarify, focus*), they, too, have acquired a conceptual orientation toward thinking about the self as an individual—along with the other conceptual baggage that goes with being a member of a community.

If we go back to Bateson's idea that relationships are really information exchanges, we can see that the student is not simply initiating, constructing, discovering, and doing all the other educationally enhancing activities associated with computing. A part of the network of relationships that make up the ecology of message exchanges we know as the classroom (including the instructional program that embodies the thought process of the program writer, teacher, other students, and the area of investigation or problem to be solved) is the message about how students are to think of themselves. It is communicated by the teacher, the epistemological assumptions and reinforcement schedule built into the software program, and the way students interact among themselves.

After observing a number of adolescents interacting with computers, Sherry Turkle, the author of *The Second Self: Computers and the Human Spirit*, concluded that "they are not concerned with whether computers might one day be like people; instead they are struck with the idea that their minds have something in common with the 'mind' of the computer before them" (1984, pp. 161–62). Her conclusion is based on descriptive accounts and long personal quotations from students who use the personal pronoun "I" and its variant expressions as a metaphor for the solitary inner world of self where feelings and ideas are worked through before serving as guides for autonomous actions and judgment. The personal references made by students, which computing reinforces, are distinctive for their lack of awareness of the self as part of an ecology of relationships: "You program yourself how to be"; "I liked the computer because I put my feelings into"; "I think of the computer as being perfect"; "The very best thing was I loved doing things my own way." Turkle concludes from this account of student self-experience that "externalization onto a canvas is a way of seeing who you are" (1984, pp. 145–153). This is indeed the point I am making here, that educational computing enters the mind by reinforcing an image of the self as autonomous and self-contained. But it is an image of self, a metaphor, that is shared within the larger culture. Having recognized that the computer amplifies certain cultural ways of understanding the nature of the self in relation to the world, we have to take the next step of acknowledging that the image of the self is culturally distinct and has an identifiable history. It can also be viewed as ideological, with roots in such early liberal thinkers as Locke, Hobbes, and Bentham.

As educational computing encourages students to accept this liberal image of the self as an autonomous and self-directing being, they will be less able to recognize how they are part of a larger cultural and natural ecology. Aside from the painful contradiction experienced as many students struggle to reconcile the image of the self as isolated, distinct, and self-contained with the pressure to conform to peer norms, the image of autonomous individualism is wrong for other reasons we have discussed earlier: membership in a language community provides a shared conceptual orientation (including, in our case, the idea of *being* a distinct individual); our sense of what is real and appropriate in terms of thought and actions is framed through the ongoing communication process with others; the concept of the self as having distinct attributes is socially formed; and, in addition to the influence of this cultural-linguistic ecology, there is also the genetic inheritance (itself influenced by cultural practices) that connects what we call the individual to the distant past.

Viewing the self as the distinctive coming together and embodiment of the cultural and biological processes does not mean we have to adopt a reductionist view that loses sight of the *individualizing* forces that gives a person's life its distinct moral, intellectual, and physical tone. Indeed, the sanctity of each person's life, each person's distinctiveness, and individual responsibility are attitudes to be highly valued. In fact, the case is being made here that an awareness of the ecology of relationships—including how the unity of culture, natural environment (the air we breathe, the plants and animals we eat, the earth we walk upon, the water we drink), and biological inheritance is given individualized expression—is essential for a deeper sense of meaning, a more adequate understanding of one's place in and contribution to sustaining our habitat, and the enhancement of mental and physical capacities.

A metaphor of self that connects us with the larger cultural and biotic community, including a sensitivity toward nourishing worthwhile traditions and a sense of responsibility for insuring that the entire ecosystem has a future, is not what is being reinforced in educational computing. Instead of fostering an awareness of the self as part of an ecological network of interdependencies and continuities in Bateson's sense, education for the Information Age fosters an egocentric universe in which decontextualized information is seen as the source of intellectual empowerment and connectedness among individuals. For the reader who thinks these statements are too general, we can easily point to the sense of drivenness that characterizes the development of computer technology itself. Although we have no understanding of how the technology will influence our political and moral relationships, traditions, and use of the habitat (will it allow for even more efficient exploitation of resources?), we push forward with what is, in fact, one experiment after another with our culture. This technological drive, of which computers are only one manifestation, is based on a view of the self and the rational process, sustained by other cultural myths pertaining to the progressive nature of change and the anthropocentric universe, that puts out of focus the importance of understanding the deeper messages about our cultural practices communicated through the rising incidence of violence, drug use, and alienation, as well as in the acid rain, the increasing loss of entire species, and the changes in weather patterns caused by the destruction of our forests. These larger message exchanges may seem far removed from students who sit in front of the microcomputer, caught up in the interaction with one of the many instructional programs and thinking of themselves as engaged in a process of data-based decision making or building their "own intellectual structure," to quote Papert again (1980, p. 32). But it is the same mind-set that ignores the importance of these relationships.

LITERACY OVER ORALITY

Although the development of computer technology is fast moving into the area of voice communication, the educational uses of microcomputers will likely remain within the technological tradition of print. Like television, which bases written scripts on market research, advances in speech-to-text capabilities is not likely to involve a shift away from a print mode of thinking and communicating. In being scripted (programmed) in advance, the wide range of voice responses will be unable to duplicate the thought process and social relationships associated with the oral tradition, which depends upon the use of shared context and nonverbal communication as important sources of meaning. This continued identification of educational computing with the mode of consciousness associated with the tradition of print (and literacy) is likely to appear to educational-computing experts as too obvious to warrant serious consideration. Indeed, their literature has been entirely silent on this aspect of cultural amplification. But what is taken for granted within the field can be viewed as evidence of the point made earlier—that thought is largely controlled by the hidden assumptions that frame the discourse, including the discourse of the educational-computing field.

A basic and long-held assumption within the educational establishment is that literacy represents the only legitimate approach to learning. In the West nonliterate people are viewed as culturally backward, lacking the basis of empowerment, and in need of learning to read and write if they are to live full and rewarding lives. This assumption is also part of the bedrock of beliefs of the educational-computing experts; it has been further buttressed by their belief that language is a neutral conduit through which senders and receivers communicate information. Print is thus viewed as a visual means of representing what is transmitted through the conduit of language, and literacy simply involves the use of the necessary encoding-decoding skills. Without rejecting the value of literacy, it is essential that we examine the arguments advanced in recent years that literacy and orality involve different forms of consciousness and thus different forms of cultural experience. Understanding the differences between the written and spoken word will help us recognize the deeper issues that must be addressed when deciding how educational computing fits within the cultural transmission process in the classroom, as well as when its use with minority cultural groups becomes a disguised form of cultural domination. The use of the microcomputer to teach reading to Native American children, according to this new line of inquiry, is not a culturally neutral experience, nor is the consciousness of the student whom Sherry Turkle views as empowered by the microcomputer left unaffected.

The eighteenth-century French philosopher Jean Jacques Rousseau was one of the first to warn against equating the written and spoken word. More recently, scholarly interest and field research have identified key differences between these modes of communication. In the 1960s, Jack Goody's (1962) fieldwork in Africa and Eric Havelock's (1963) examination of the changes in Greek consciousness that followed the shift from the spoken to written word represented a pioneering effort. During the last decade, the investigations of Walter Ong (1977, 1982), Ronald and Suzanne Scollon (1985), and Sylvia Scribner and Michael Cole (1981), among others, have focused on institutional (i.e., schools) and cultural variables. Their research, taken as a whole, raises important questions about the continuation of the educational practice of privileging literacy over orality by assuming that the written word is a more reliable source of knowledge.

Walter Ong, a seminal scholar in the field, makes the following observation about the change from a predominantly oral to literate tradition:

> It would appear that the technological inventions of writing, print, and electronic verbalization, in their historical effects, are connected with and have helped bring about a certain kind of alienation within the human life world. This is not at all to say that these inventions have been simply destructive, but rather they have restructured consciousness, affecting men's and women's presence to the world and to themselves and creating new interior distances within the psyche. (1977, p. 1)

How the educational use of computers, with their dependence on print technology, contributes to this alienating process can be seen in how the printed word involves a different pattern of relationships from those we experience through the spoken word. In the summary that follows it is important not to confuse the spoken word with the machine-activated voice, as the latter involves the procedural thinking of a program.

Literacy contributes to two basic forms of modern alienation—what the Scollons (1985) refer to as the separation of the word from the body (the reification of the printed word) and separation in our personal relationships. The privileged status given literacy since it was made a primary mission of public schools has prevented a critical examination of what is involved when the printed word is viewed as the primary carrier of authoritative knowledge. As Ong points out, we confer a special status on the printed word and distrust the spoken word:

> Writing makes 'words' appear similar to things because we think of words as visible marks signaling words to decoders: we can see and

> touch such inscribed 'words' in texts and books. Written words are residue. Oral tradition has no such visual residue or deposit. (1982, p. 11)

The printed word thus begins to be viewed as more real than the transitory quality of personal experience—taste, touch, smell, sight, and the spoken word. By way of contrast, the printed word takes on a unique sense of reality and authority that endures over time.

This reordering of our psychic space, where the abstraction of the printed word becomes more real than the experience that it signifies, is further strengthened by how literacy alters human relationships. The acceptance of the abstract written word as being more real than experience itself is complemented by the alienation that literacy fosters between persons. Writing—whether it takes the form of an article, novel, or instructional program—separates the sender from the receiver, turning communication, as the Scollons observe, into an asymmetrical power relationship (1985, p. 19). The writer and reader do not stand in an immediate relationship that allows for reciprocal communication. Instead, the writer and reader must enter into a highly privatized world wherein the writer transmits and the reader receives and reflects on the message. For the writer it is a matter of having the quiet and isolation that allows thoughts to be formulated and communicated in a linear and decontextualized manner, and directed toward an abstract audience or public that must be accurately predicted if communication is to occur. The reader must also enter the privatized world that allows for full engagement in the process of abstract thought; that is, to follow the linear pattern of thought constructed by the author and to reflect upon it. Unlike the ongoing flow of oral communication, which depends so heavily upon the use of context and paralinguistic signals as part of the message exchange, writing involves a fixed text and thus allows for analysis as different texts are compared. The term used in connection with understanding the nonneutrality of technology applies here; as a technology print amplifies an autonomous sense of individualism (the isolating nature of writing and reading) and analytical thought.

The connection between reading and analytical thought can be seen in the original meaning of the Greek word *theoria,* which meant looking at, viewing from a distance, and contemplation. Analytical thought involves this mental distancing, which is facilitated through print. Ironically, the fixed nature of the text, which provides the needed reference points for analysis, also means that the content is no longer part of lived experience. Ong observes that people who are educated to use the codes (that is, who are literate) can "reconstruct real words in externalized sound or in their auditory imaginations." He goes on to note that "most persons in technological cultures are strongly conditioned . . . to assume that the printed word is the real word, and the spoken word is inconsequential. Permanent unreality is more plausible and comforting than reality that is transient" (1977, p. 21).

Unlike the printed word, which must be decoded (an ability now largely learned in public schools where literacy is taught as part of an ideological package), the spoken word is the natural means of communicating about a living relationship. It also involves acquiring the conceptual categories that organize thought and social behavior into shared patterns, but it differs from the printed word in fundamentally important ways. The Scollons' quotation of an old Navajo woman's statement—"Separate the word from the body. That's death"—goes to the heart of the difference between the written and spoken word (1985, p. 2). When the word becomes an object (as in print), it falsifies our most basic relationships. As the Scollons put it, "the word comes to take precedence over the situation, analysis takes precedence over participation, isolated thought takes precedence over conversation and story telling, and the individual takes precedence over the community" (1985, p. 10).

Their statement points to the way in which print (including the electronically formatted print of the computer) "enters the mind, producing new states of awareness there," to quote Ong (1977, p. 47). The spoken word involves a participatory relationship and thus is the living bond that sustains the sense of community. It also involves all the senses in a learning process that is real, contextual, and dynamic. Although the oral tradition often utilizes formulaic knowledge—conceptual formulas, fixed sayings—the spoken word is more adaptable to communicating knowledge that is vital to lives of the community; and as Jack Goody (1977) noted from his studies of African oral cultures, knowledge communicated through the spoken word is continually updated to fit the changing circumstances of community life. The dynamic nature of the spoken word, which is sustained through remembering rather than memorizing, leads many in literate society to view the spoken word as less trustworthy than the written word. But the great irony is that the written word takes on even more authority as context and authorship are lost sight of. Another basic difference is that the narrative tradition of the spoken word involves the sharing of analogue knowledge—the stories that contain the conceptual and moral templates (the redundant elements of culture) that have evolved through a testing process of many generations and serve as the guidelines for life in the community.

The basic differences between the spoken and written word—the former involving participatory relationships and the use of language to communicate about the living (present) word, the latter fostering isolation, abstract thought, and the reification of the word—might lead many to adopt the romantic position in which literacy is viewed as the basic source of our problems. What is being urged here is not the abolition of the printed word, but rather the recognition that the two modes of communication are fundamentally different, as well as an understanding of the cultural and personal consequences that follow when either mode, within the context of our society, is given a privileged standing. In terms of broad curricular policies this understanding should lead to a more conscious effort to balance the educational methodologies that use the printed word (books, microcomputers, printed materials) with ones that use the spoken word (storytelling, oral history—including the epic narratives of the dominant and minority cultures).

This concern with balancing the written and spoken word, and thus giving legitimacy to the latter, also has specific implications for thinking about the educational uses of microcomputers. The connection between educational computing and the technological culture of print further supports the arguments that computers are not a neutral technology that simply expand our ability to store and manipulate information. In effect, the privileging of print over orality means that the use of microcomputers strengthens certain cultural patterns and orientations and weakens others. Educational computing thus involves both educational and political questions that must be addressed by classroom teachers as well as the people who write the instructional software programs and provide guidance on how to incorporate the technology into the classroom. As our brief summary of the differences between literacy and orality makes problematic the myth of progress so essential to developments in educational computing, we can no longer limit ourselves to a sole concern with procedural questions of how to use the technology in a more efficient manner. The real questions are, How does educational computing fit into the socialization process, and what professional judgments should the teacher be prepared to make? We shall now take up these questions in a more direct manner, hoping that all the people involved in the advancement of educational computing—directors at the school-district level, people who write the instructional software, professors of educational computing who influence how prospective teachers view the use of the technology, and corporate promoters—will see the importance of reframing what constitutes expertise in the educational uses of the microcomputer.

CHAPTER 4

The Teacher's Responsibility for the Recovery of the Symbolic World

There have been rapid developments in the technology of artificial intelligence that will inevitably be hailed by educational-computer experts as essential to instructional use, developments that range from natural language processing that will allow students to communicate with the computer in English to new applications of visual imaging. These advances stand in sharp contrast to the lack of progress in understanding the responsibility of the teacher for insuring that the use of microcomputers makes a genuine contribution to the education of students. This point is missed by the euphoric teacher who declared that "in the Apple Classroom of Tomorrow, we enjoy living every computer educator's dream of unlimited computer access for each of our students" and by the director of computer education for the school district in which the ACOT classroom is located who asserted that "connecting students with computers won't disconnect them from their regular programs. We won't mess with what's going to be learned, just some of the teaching tools will be different" (the "teaching tools" were referred to as "electronic pencils") (Caley, 1986, p. 38; "Computer," 1987, p. 1C). I heard a similar lack of understanding of the core issues expressed by a teacher at a recent educational-computing conference in British Columbia. Translating his deeply felt sense of personal vulnerability into a bit of sage advice for other teachers to consider, he warned that "if you are the type of person who wants to know more than your students, don't teach computers. They'll out distance you in a couple of weeks." In contrast to this teacher, who understood the problem of power but not his professional role in the cultural transmission process, the promoters of educational computing fill the conceptual vacuum with procedural advice on how to integrate the microcomputer into every area of the curriculum—including the writing of poetry.

But the procedural information of how to use *AppleWorks* to organize and manage spelling instruction or how to simulate the pattern of thinking of the professional historian, to cite just two examples, is not the same as understanding the judgments that every competent teacher should be able to make. This is not to say that learning the procedural thinking required to unlock the use of an instructional software program is not, in its own way, intellectually challenging to the teacher. The point, rather, is that education is far more complex than using a microcomputer to process and manipulate information, or even to enter the supposedly conceptually open world of LOGO. When conducted within the setting of a classroom, education is supposed to be guided, at least within the context of our culture, by a set of values and assumptions about what constitutes a contribution to society as well as about the nature of individual empowerment. It also is guided by concerns that reflect a sensitivity, variously informed by folk knowledge and critical judgment, to the lessons of the past that are to be avoided or repeated. Education in the classroom is also caught up in the cross-currents of commercial hype, interest-group politics, and the growing disjuncture between technological development and moral insight. But beyond the "no school is an island" argument, there are dynamic cultural processes within the classroom that influence the outcome of the educational process. These processes, involving the interaction between the historically rooted symbolic systems that provide the patterns that guide thought, nonverbal communication, and the allocation of cultural resources that will influence the student's later standing, go largely unrecognized. When not understood, the symbolic reproduction process can lead to a form of education that severely limits conscious choice and result in strengthening the more problematic aspects of cultural development that were identified in Chapter 1. On the other hand, when the teacher understands the nature of the cultural transmission process, as well as possesses a sensitivity to the cultural patterns that are life enhancing, formal education can make a genuine contribution to meeting the ongoing challenge of cultural renewal. Unfortunately, schooling appears to contribute as much to the more destructive cultural practices as it does to the more desirable ones. Because neither the larger cultural-political context within which the school is situated nor the dynamics of cultural transmission within the classroom are addressed by the people who control the discourse within the field of educational computing, this double-bind is unlikely to be alleviated by the advances in educational computing. The 1987 National Educational Computing Conference serves as a good example of the narrow procedural thinking that dominates the field. More than 150 papers were presented, and only two dealt with topics other than the more technical aspects of educational computing. One dealt with the problem of gender, and the other was a paper I presented on "Teaching a 19th-Century Mode of Thinking Through a 20th-Century Machine."

Technological consciousness, so evident at this conference and more generally in the literature on educational computing, appears to be driven by a need for greater power to predict and control; it also is associated with the pursuit of materialistic values. The hubris of this mind-set, which can also be viewed as a form of cultural elitism, stands in sharp contrast to Wendell Berry's view of how we must bring a sense of balance to our lives. Proponents who think I have misread all the progressive values that are reinforced through educational computing should ponder whether the following statement by Berry can be reconciled with their own technocratic view of cultural progress:

> A healthy culture is a communal order of memory, insight, value, work, conviviality, reverence, aspiration. It reveals the human necessities and human limits. It clarifies our inescapable bonds to the earth and to each other. It assures that the necessary restraints are observed, and that the work is done, and that it is done well. (1986, p. 43)

Berry is referring here to values that strengthen community, meaningful traditions, a personal sense of work that is ecologically sound and socially useful, and the awareness of the interdependency of all forms of life. Such an outlook stands in contrast to the technocratic mind-set, which is based on many of the cultural assumptions embraced by Papert and Tom Snyder, two of the more reflective thinkers within the field. The following statement has simply omitted, in the name of efficiency, their concern with mobilizing the "conceptual potential" of the individual:

> In the past humans were both translators and transmitters of information: the operator was the ultimate interface between design intent . . . and machine function. The human used mental and physical abilities to control machines. Today however, computers are increasingly becoming the translators and transmitters of information, and numerical control is perhaps most representative of the kind of control that plugs into that stream with a minimum of human intervention. The manufacturing industry is favoring the purchase of machines with controls that require

> less operator attention to oversee the process. It talks of machine tools with sophisticated automatic controls that will work in groups with two-way communication with higher level computers. . . . It does not seem likely that, in the hierarchical system contemplated the operator will exercise much judgment. (quoted in Noble, 1984, p. 328)

This is a remarkable statement, as it reveals the contradiction that underlies the field of educational computing—with its tendency to utilize traditional humanistic values to justify the increasing integration of technology into the educational process.

While most advocates of educational computing see only the positive side of the Information Age being ushered in by the new technology, other observers warn about the danger of de-skilling factory and office employers. Similarly their naive understanding of the connection between computer technology and ideology stands in sharp contrast to critics who argue that developing a technology that benefits management at the expense of workers is dangerously short-sighted. "The schools need to teach their engineers how to design machines that work with human interaction built in—not cut out" (Clayton, 1987, p. 22). But when so few teachers and educational computing experts understand the interconnection between technology and political choices, or seem unwilling to think deeply about the negative side of the Information Age, there is little chance that the conceptual foundations will be laid for understanding the complex cultural issues surrounding the idea that technology should be designed to enhance the well-being of the person and community, an undertaking that involves contributing to both the quality of social relationships and the enhancement of a person's skills. The optimists who see a social and educational inevitability about preparing for life in the Information Age should also consider whether the military use of this technology has improved our margin of safety or reduced it. They might also consider the dangers to our civil liberties brought about by the development of high-tech surveillance systems that collect information on all aspects of citizens' lives and allow for the sharing of this information among different branches of the government (including intelligence agencies) and private industry (Siegel and Markoff, 1985, p. 41).

One possible reason why there is so little discussion about the broader social implications of educational computing has to do with the acceptance of the assumption that individuals must be prepared to process massive amounts of information if they are to make rational decisions. This assumption about autonomous individuals faced with a many-layered world of data makes the computer appear to be a latter-day Promethean gift, as basic to the continuation of social existence as the original gift of fire. This generative metaphor of the human condition, which also represents educational computing as teaching "the basics of an age [students] are entering," is clearly stated by Pamela McCorduck in her book, *The Universal Machine: Confessions of a Technological Optimist*. The educational use of computers, she claims, addressing what she sees as the minimum benefits,

> teaches *process*, a dynamic way of dealing with *intellectual abstractions* over time, unbounded by the circumstances of any given set of facts but adaptable to *new facts, new data, change*. Well-structured problems that would require children to use a variety of computing tools at appropriate places would teach perhaps the most valuable skill of all, which is *problem solving*. Beyond that, students acquire the confidence to deal with *complexity*, for even the simplest programs can transform a certain degree of messy, muddy detail into more clearly structured *intellectual representations*. (1985, p. 229; italics added)

The social world is represented here as in a continual process of change, and it is only through an abstract grasp of the segmented parts (facts, data, information) that it can be given a sense of order. The conclusion that follows from this view is that the continual process of problem solving requires greater reliance on the use of computers.

The ideal form of education, according to this view, would be the "computer-saturated classroom," as represented in the experimental ACOT classrooms. McCorduck also found the ideal being expressed in the thinking of Andries van Dam, a professor of computer science at Brown University. If he has his way, she writes, "and scholars' workstations (or students' computers) are connected to each other usefully, then their lucky users will also learn the power of collaborative intellectual effort, which is *community* in the best sense" (1985, p. 230). Aside from the fact that McCorduck's way of thinking is typical of the field, the real significance of her statement lies in what is revealed about the form of individualism and community that is reinforced through the use of computers.

AWARENESS OF GENDER BIAS

In Chapter 1 it was suggested that one aspect of the cultural crisis we face relates to how the liberal view of individualism and the community (including nonhuman life forms) are to be reconciled. The argument was made there that the liberal emphasis on individual empowerment and self-direction, along with an ever-shifting coalition approach to interest-group politics, lacks the essential commitment to preserve the interests of the larger community. The view of how the individual experiences community in McCorduck's statement puts in focus the cultural orientation toward individualism that is fostered by the "hurry-up" characteristics of educational computing. Perhaps even more interesting in terms of recent research on language and gender is the connection between educational computing and the dominant Western male view of individualism.

Intelligence is seen by all the educational computer experts quoted here (Papert, Snyder, and so forth) as individualistic in nature; and its highest expression is viewed as involving procedural thinking, whereby the data and simulations are to be dealt with at an abstract, decontextualized level. The values to be achieved through educational computing, in addition to self-expression, include efficiency, an ever-increasing capacity for problem solving, and an increase in power over an external and chaotic world that must be brought under rational control. The experience of computing also includes, in addition to the above, the patterns of thought and social relationships associated with print—the writing and reading process that involves physical isolation (even when surrounded by other people who are also attending to the monitor), communicating by way of digital signals that encode the data that is to be shared with others (McCorduck's ideal of community), and the encounter of the mind with the printed word that is disconnected from human authorship.

As we have dealt in the first chapter with the chief characteristics of the liberal view of the individual who, in being free of the authority of tradition, must continually re-establish authority anew on the basis of data, it would be useful to shift the argument in a way that puts in focus the relationship between educational computing and the problem of gender dominance in our society. This shift in focus, however, simply provides another way of understanding the interconnection that exists between the form of consciousness orientated toward technological development, regardless of impact on the cultural-natural ecology, and the privileging of a masculine over a feminine way of knowing (Keller, 1985).

Social linguists, such as Robin Lakoff (1975) and Deborah Tannen (1986), have found that differences in conversational styles between American men and women reflect deeper divisions in value orientation and ways of thinking. Although ethnicity and regional differences always lead to qualifying generalizations about gender differences, they nevertheless found that women are more attuned to the importance of relationships in communication. Men, on the other hand, tend to view communication as a conduit for the sending and receiving of information needed for problem solving. Women rely more on analogic knowledge, wherein meaning and pattern have antecedents in the past, while men have been socialized to be more comfortable in the Cartesian world of observation, measurement, and the accumulation of "objective" facts (Bordo, 1987). Although men cannot escape metaphorical thinking, they tend not to value it as a source of collective memory that could be used as a guide to future experience. There are also differences in conversational styles, with men being more attuned to the linear construction of a conversation as well as to a conversational rhythm that avoids the appearance of hesitancy (and thus of not being in control) (Tannen and Saville-Troike, 1985).

These differences in cognitive and communication style also carry through to differences in value orientation. And again the evidence suggests that the computer is not a gender-neutral technology. In her book *In a Different Voice,* Carol Gilligan summarizes the differences that emerged as men and women from the dominant cultural group described themselves as persons and how they fit into the larger scheme of things. The most distinctive difference, according to Gilligan's findings, is that women define themselves in terms of relationships, with a strong emphasis on the importance of responsibility, care, and nurturing (Gilligan, 1982). The self-descriptions of men, on the other hand, involve the use of adjectives that represent a different conceptual and moral stance. The personal qualities emphasized ("intelligent," "logical," "imaginative," "honest") suggest a way of thinking about the self that does not need to be supported by relationships. The sense of being responsible primarily to oneself for the full realization of an inner, individualistic potential, which Gilligan found in the interview data, represents the male ideal that has been celebrated in the West as the ideological standard against which all individuals (both female and male) were to judge themselves. T. S. Eliot seems to have captured the basic difference that emerges in Gilligan's research findings when he wrote, "We had the experience but missed the meaning,/And approach to the meaning restores the experience. . . ." And further on in the same poem he expressed the thought "That the past experience revived in the meaning/Is not the experience of one life only . . . " (Eliot, 1943, p. 39).

Meanings are deepened by a sensitivity to relationships; relationships are the content of memory; and memory is what makes experience shared rather than isolating and individualistic. Gilligan's research and Eliot's ability to escape the conceptual recipes of a male-constructed ideology take us back to the conceptual differences between analogue and digital knowledge. This is also the connection point between educational computing and the unresolved problem of gender dominance. Interaction with a microcomputer involves a person-machine relationship, not an interpersonal one of sharing, nurturing, and caring. The person-machine relationship, at its best, involves the refining of ideas through the manipulation of data and abstract visual representations. At its worst, it is processing abstract information in order to establish the "truth" about an equally abstract aspect of social life that is perceived as requiring a technical response. However, beyond the Kafkaesque world of data processing so brilliantly represented in Terry Gilliam's film *Brazil*, there is the male thought pattern that users must interact with.

In the case of women, this involves reconciling their own sense of integrity about what is intellectually and morally important with the conceptual and value-laden agenda that males have designed into the computer. The concern with efficiency, power, abstractions, and logic, as well as the sheer mechanical aspects of mastering all the commands of a program, reflects the hubris of the "autonomous male" (who can exist only in the realm of ideology) who uses data to construct a more rationally ordered world. An example of this decontextualized pattern of thinking can be seen in the *Max Think* software program, which promises to make available to educational users "55 different conceptual ways of thinking." The "high-level thinking" facilitated by this program turns out to be procedures for processing information: "How to expand information," "How to organize information," "How to process information." The other categories relating to how power is derived from the effective handling of information are summarized by the terms *manage, examine, use, create,* and *get more out of existing information* (*Max Think,* 1986, pp. 141–142). While the producers of educational software are reducing meaning and relationships to information, Larry Snarr (director of the National Center for Supercomputing Applications at the University of Illinois) offers a different and even more disturbing view of the future:

> The ultimate in the new technology will be a computer system so fast and so powerful that it will be able to compute the output of a supercomputer directly into the eye-brain system. The human at this point will become the limiting factor in the computer cycle. . . . The distinction between artificial and real reality will begin to be hard to perceive simply by looking at it. (quoted in "Numbers Crunch In," 1987, p. E1)

Although it would be a fundamental error to assume that the cognitive style of men reduces all aspects of relationships to nothing more than information, it would be difficult to see how a predominantly analogic pattern of thinking, where pattern, continuity, meaning, and identity merge as the basis of understanding the new in terms of the familiar, could have produced the *Max Think* program or envisaged the human as the weak link in the computer cycle. To paraphrase Dale Spender, it has to be understood as the "male version of reality" and thus as only a "partial view of the world" (1984, p. 195).

The many books and journals that promote educational computing primarily address the technical questions and thus use the language that represents the problem-solving, achievement orientation that is more associated with the male view of reality. As a result, classroom teachers, as well as the general public, have not been given the language necessary to articulate the issues relating to how developments in computer technology have altered human relationships and values. To use Gilligan's term, the most important question about this new technology has to do with relationships: our relationships with each other, with the natural environment, and the implications of these relationships for the inner world of the individual where the problems of alienation, meaning, and connectedness have to be resolved. The problem of relationships is the major professional issue facing the classroom teacher. But the language of educational computing has put this out of focus, causing the nontechnologically-oriented teacher to feel backward and out of step with the new technology of the Information Age.

Although the real power of teachers to affect directly the process of cultural change is limited, they cannot avoid participating in the dynamics at work in the larger society. In each shift of the dominant consciousness, on issues relating to literacy, race, and gender, teachers have adjusted both classroom conversation and curriculum materials to fit their interpretation of the new social consensus. Teachers face a similar situation with regard to the connection between educational computing and the cultural changes that will result from this technology. But unlike changes related to race and gender, the consensus will be more difficult to interpret. As the multibillion-dollar computer industry uses the media to represent itself as serving the highest interest of humanity, there remains the highly visible evidence of wasted and impoverished lives, a growing imbalance in social power and wealth, and the accelerating deterioration in the physical environment. Unlike the straightforward nature of the issues connected with racism and gender, those surrounding the new technology make it more difficult for the average teacher to determine whether the computer is part of the solution or part of the problem. But regardless of whether they downplay educational computing out of fear of the technology, as in the case of the teacher who was concerned with remaining in control, or accept the vision of the future represented in the buzz words *Information Age*, what they do in the classroom will contribute to a collective state of consciousness. The real issue is whether this state of consciousness will involve an awareness of the questions that must be asked about the benefits of this new technology and the direction in which we are moving as a culture, or whether it will involve the acceptance of computers as a necessary and inevitable aspect of progress. The knowledge required for helping students become more reflective about how computer technology—or, for that matter, any other technology—fits into the moral ecology of relationships is not acquired by learning how to use the instructional potential of a software program. As expertise in educational computing does not encompass this domain of understanding, the teachers will have to acquire it elsewhere. Among other things, teachers will need to recognize their own areas of professional responsibility rather than yielding to the feeling of being powerless and irrelevant because they are not as skilled in computer mechanics as their students.

CONSCIOUSNESS RAISING

Teachers have a unique set of responsibilities in the educational process, but because of a faulty set of assumptions about the nature of the individual, language, and the learning process, the literature on educational computing—mostly "how-to" articles, books, and manuals—has trivialized these responsibilities by reducing the teacher to a facilitator who is to be guided by a set of technical concerns. We encountered examples of this technological orientation in earlier chapters in looking at the practical guidelines laid out for teachers to follow in choosing a software program. The following guideline represents the same procedural thinking and encompasses the same misconceptions about the nature of the educational process:

> If the teacher is to play an active role in focusing on skills and strategies, then the *teacher* must be interacting with students and the computer. To teach thinking skills, such teacher direction is essential. A 25-inch monitor for the students, one computer, and a small monitor for the teacher is an appropriate arrangement. The teacher can then run the program and

ROSZAK – EMPHASIZE IDEAS NOT INFORMATION!

PRINCIPAL TASK of EDUCATION is to teach young MINDS HOW to DEAL WITH IDEAS; how to evaluate them, extend and ADAPT them.

Thinking is not collecting information!.

direct the instruction, focusing on the targeted thinking skills, labeling those skills, and increasing the probability of transfer.

Appropriate software can help the teacher create a manageable environment to focus on thinking. The following criteria can assist in choosing this software:

—Does the software focus on significant thinking skills as its objective?
—Are there multiple levels of difficulty so that the teacher can adjust to students' needs?
—Are there multiple solutions which vary in sophistication?
—Does the software have multiple problems so that it can be used repeatedly?
—Is the software designed for a cooperative, non-competitive environment?

> Most software designed to teach thinking skills does so within a specific situation that can be effectively modeled with the computer. . . . Avoid the assumption that software teaches. It is the teacher who teaches; the software is only the medium. (Van Deusen and Donham, 1986–87, p. 32)

Papert also refers to the computer as a medium that fosters the development of independent thinking and assigns to the teacher the same facilitating role. But he makes several other popular misconceptions a more central part of his rationale for LOGO. Language, for Papert, provides the means for communicating individual ideas; it is also seen as expanding the student's imagination and perception (but just how this is done is not explained). This conduit view of language complements, indeed is required by, his belief that "the knowledge that you have is something you make" (quoted in Reinhold, 1986, p. 35). Concern about the content of the curriculum—that is, the specific ideas and values students are being asked to learn—is noticeably absent in the above quotations. By viewing the classroom through the outdated ideological lenses of the past, the proponents of educational computing, in effect, end up representing the teacher's responsibilities in a way that strengthens the connections between schooling and a technological social order.

Again, we face the task of reframing how the learning processes in the classroom should be understood. If we start with the language of anthropology and the sociology of knowledge rather than the mélange that educators have borrowed from various traditions of nineteenth-century liberal thought, we find the teacher being confronted with an entirely different set of responsibilities. The classroom, according to this alternative way of understanding, should be viewed as part of a complex language process whereby adults are attempting to pass on to students the cultural patterns, norms, and procedures for thinking and interacting with others. Clifford Geertz provides a useful way of thinking about what is being learned as teacher and students participate in the message-exchange processes that characterize the classroom:

> Once human behavior is seen as . . . symbolic action—action which, like phonation in speech, pigment in painting, line in writing, or sonance in music signifies—the question as to whether culture is patterned conduct or a frame of mind, or even the two somehow mixed together, loses sense. (1973, p. 10)

As he implies, culture is both as public as behavior and as private as meaning; it is also both explicit and implicit. But most important, it encompasses the humanly created world and is shared, sustained, and reinterpreted (according to Homer Barnett, also misinterpreted) through the processes of communication, both verbal and nonverbal. The interconnection between individual consciousness, language, and culture should not, it must be reiterated, be taken to the extreme of viewing the individual entirely as the expression of culture. The loss of the sharp boundary separation between individual and culture, thought and language, does not mean that the individual lacks the ability to give personal, even unique, expression to the cultural forms into which thought and behavior are fitted. Continuities and connectedness, rather than distinct entities and events, should be the basis of understanding. Following Bateson's lead, this means paying attention to the fundamental role that communication plays in providing the symbolic milieu within which the individual orients and gives expression to the self.

THE NATURE OF PRIMARY SOCIALIZATION

The classroom can be understood as an exceedingly complex process of communication, involving oral and written message exchanges, the use of space and body language, and paralinguistic elements—use of pauses, changes in tone, and intensity of voice. In addition to sustaining the cultural patterns and norms (which have been learned and subsequently function mostly at a taken-for-granted level of understanding), the classroom also involves learning new elements of, as well as variations on, the collective belief system—what Geertz calls the matrices of a collective consciousness, the "extrapersonal mechanisms for perception, understanding, judgment, and manipulation of the world" (1973, p. 216). The learning of new elements—which include what to value, how to think about the interconnections in experience (or the disconnections, such as facts and data), what the appropriate behaviors and expectations are, and the areas of experience that are out of bounds in terms of serious thought—represents primary socialization. Since much of the curriculum (both materials and teacher talk) is intended to introduce students to aspects of the culture they have not experienced directly or learned to think about formally, the teacher can be viewed as engaged in primary socialization. That is, the teacher is playing a unique gatekeeper role that can have a powerful influence on the development of the student's conceptual map (ability to interpret and make one's way through or around the cultural patterns within which everyday experience is organized), self-concept, and life chances within the political-economic system.

Understanding the dynamics of this gatekeeper role, which characterizes the teacher's involvement in primary socialization, will take us a considerable distance toward identifying the professional judgments teachers must be able to exercise when microcomputers are used to introduce students to new material or are used in a manner that reinforces the taken-for-granted cultural knowledge learned elsewhere. The identification of the teacher's responsibilities will represent a different set of educational priorities from those we find in either the earlier statement on teaching thinking skills or Papert's supposedly more emancipatory approach, which he sees as "opposed to our current educational model in which knowledge is transferred from a teacher's head to a student's head" (quoted in Reinhold, 1986, p. 35).

But before we examine more closely what the teacher should be aware of as the process of primary socialization evolves, it is essential that we identify the critically important distinction between learning the culture at the implicit and explicit levels, as well as how the relationship between language acquisition and explicit knowledge relate to the development of communicative competence. These are distinctions that have been overlooked by the promoters of educational computing, as well as by educational psychologists, who, in developing their theories about individual intelligence, have ignored both the way in which culture is learned and the metaphorical nature of thought.

The anthropologist Mary Douglas makes the point that the implicit knowledge we possess of cultural norms, patterns, and procedures (the shared information codes passed down from the past) is "regarded as too true to warrant discussion" (1975, p. 4). This taken-for-granted knowledge (experienced as part of our natural attitude, e.g., the automatic change in body language to fit social context and message) provides, according to Douglas,

> the necessary unexamined assumptions upon which ordinary discourse takes place. Its stability is an illusion, for a large part of discourse is dedicated to creating, revising and obliquely affirming this implicit background, without ever directing explicit attention upon it. When the background of assumptions upholds what is verbally explicit, meanings come across loud and clear. Through these implicit channels of meaning, human society itself is achieved, clarity and speed of clue-reading ensured. (1975, p.4)

But while this background of taken-for-granted knowledge remains stable, thus allowing for the appropriateness of the explicit knowledge to be negotiated, Douglas points to the dynamic interplay between implicit (backgrounding) and explicit (foregrounding) knowledge: "In the exclusive exchange between explicit and implicit meanings a perceived-to-be regular universe establishes itself precariously, shifts, topples and sets itself up again" (1975, p. 4).

The interplay between the stability of background knowledge, parts of which may be made explicit and reworked, and the other patterns that are the focus of our explicit attention can be seen in the ongoing process of developing a more gender-neutral language. In the past, sexist language was taken for granted, as were the social practices and norms it dictated. The process of making the taken-for-granted explicit occurred, as Douglas notes, against a background of other cultural assumptions and patterns that remained stable (e.g., relating change with progress, authority with critical reflection, and individualism with freedom). Similarly, innovations in computer technology led to making explicit traditional classroom expectations and practices; but as new meanings were negotiated, much of the background knowledge (the cultural assumptions relating to writing left to right, top to bottom on the page, the nature of a fact, concern with efficiency, and a problem-solving approach to thinking) remained "too true to warrant discussion." It remained as part of the background of taken-for-granted knowledge.

Douglas's representation of the interplay of implicit (tacit) and explicit knowledge involves a second connection that needs to be understood by the teacher, who plays a key role in orchestrating the process of primary socialization. As we have learned in the past few years, the naming of sexist social practices was essential to removing them from the realm of stable, taken-for-granted background knowledge; in being named, the practices were made explicit and thus could be thought about in a more critical way. Although the naming process also involves a continuing interplay of implicit assumptions and explicit awareness, it puts in focus what is to be given thoughtful attention. But as Schon (1979) observes, language does not provide an objective way of representing what is; rather its metaphorical nature provides the conceptual models (interpretative frameworks) that influence how relationships will be understood. Thus even the process of critical reflection is framed by other cultural assumptions (background knowledge) that are unconsciously held.

Without getting involved in all the complexities and nuances that characterize the connections among culture, language, and thought, we can move ahead by summarizing the essentials of how language relates to communicative competence. Taken-for-granted knowledge leads to the re-enactment of cultural patterns at an unconscious level, such as following the cultural norms for establishing eye contact with others. When individuals lack the language (vocabulary, including the generative metaphors that provide the conceptual frameworks necessary for organizing ideas in a coherent way) to make this knowledge explicit, there is little possibility that communication with others will lead to negotiating new meanings and relationships—which is the essence of the political process. The possession of a complex language code, one that provides the lexical means of representing the complexity of experience—including the interconnection between explicit and implicit understandings—is essential to being able to enter into the process of negotiating with others a new set of patterns for organizing experience. Without the language code necessary for reflection and reinterpretation, they will be dependent upon those who possess the linguistic ability to rename (reframe) the problematic areas of social experience. Possession of a complex language does not determine all political outcomes (although a case could be made that it will be used to legitimate political decisions determined by other means), but it is related, at least within our society, to an individual's communicative competence in the political realm, where the guiding cultural patterns are being renegotiated. Put simply, if individuals cannot articulate what they understand as the relevant issues they will not be able to participate effectively in the negotiation process.

The process of primary socialization, wherein the student is learning something for the first time, involves the same interconnections of past knowledge learned at both the implicit and explicit levels.

It also involves acquiring the language that will serve as the initial conceptual scaffolding for new understandings, as well as what can be explicitly (consciously) communicated to others. Primary socialization thus can be seen as a process of conceptual mapmaking, wherein the significant other (such as a teacher, textbook, or instructional software program) communicates to the person undergoing socialization the patterns and information codes that help to organize experience into socially coherent and accepted ways. For example, when students use a microcomputer they undergo primary socialization; along with the new factual information communicated through the instructional software program, they also acquire or have reinforced the cultural assumptions embedded in computer technology—assumptions about the efficacy of procedural thinking, the reification of the printed word, the sense of community as being realized through the sharing of information, and the progressive nature of educational computing.

CHANGING THE DYNAMICS OF PRIMARY SOCIALIZATION

Unlike the guidelines for using the microcomputer to teach "thinking skills," the view of primary socialization presented here puts in focus the cultural content of the message exchange that occurs as students and teacher interact with the instructional software program. The content, represented in the natural language that appears on the monitor screen, is what adds to or reinforces the students' conceptual framework. Both the nature of the content and the manner in which it is learned will have an impact on their thought process and their growth in communicative competence. This is the area of teacher responsibility that is ignored by the advocates of educational computing, who have reduced education to learning a set of procedures for acquiring and manipulating data. In effect, they have limited human intelligence to the idea of the mind that is embedded in the technology, a point that concerns Theodore Roszak. Since we are dealing here with the question of what constitutes the teacher's responsibility in relation to the educational use of microcomputers, it is important to restate Roszak's fuller criticism. In *The Cult of Information*, Roszak warns:

> Introducing students to the computer at an early age, creating the impression that their little exercises in programming and game playing are somehow giving them control over a powerful technology, can be a dangerous deception. It is not teaching them to think in a scientifically sound way; it is persuading them to acquiesce. It is accustoming them to

> the presence of computers in every walk of life, and thus making them dependent upon the machine's supposed necessity and superiority. (1986, p. 218)

Socialization to a particular pattern of thinking as well as to the assumptions about the superiority of the technology over the human mind can be seen in a program for writing poetry that goes by the name of *Compupoem*. It is presented here as an example of primary socialization that requires a different set of responses on the part of the teacher from those represented in the teacher guides to educational computing. *Compupoem*, according to William Wresch, demonstrates the "ways the computer can bring out the poet in all children" (1985, p. 124). Again, the assumption is made that the procedural thinking of the program unlocks a potential within the student that otherwise might not have been discovered or if discovered by some other means would not have been developed as efficiently. We shall follow the *Compupoem* program procedures necessary for the "creation" of the student's first poem:

> THIS GAME CAN HELP YOU
> BECOME A POET.
>
> YOU WIN THE GAME IF YOU WRITE
> SOMETHING YOU LIKE OR IF YOU HAVE
> AN INTERESTING TIME.
>
> PLEASE FOLLOW THE DIRECTIONS
> BELOW—AND SEE HOW LONG
> IT TAKES TO LEARN THE
> GAME'S RULES.
>
> FIRST: THINK OF A NOUN, ANY NOUN . . .
>
> (COMPUTERS CAN'T READ MINDS—YET.)
>
> WHAT'S YOUR NOUN? *SNOW*
>
> WHAT'S AN ADJECTIVE
> THAT DESCRIBES YOUR NOUN? *EVER-FALLING*
>
> WHAT'S ANOTHER ADJECTIVE
> DESCRIBING YOUR NOUN? *BLINDING*
>
> WHAT'S A PREPOSITIONAL PHRASE
> THAT "PUTS" YOUR NOUN SOMEPLACE? *ON WISCONSIN*
>
> WHAT'S A VERB THAT DESCRIBES WHAT
> YOUR NOUN MIGHT DO THERE, OR
> HOW IT MIGHT BE? *DROPPING*

HOW ABOUT AN ADVERB THAT MODIFIES
THAT VERB? *HEAVILY*

(YOU'RE ALMOST DONE.)

THINK OF ONE MORE ADVERB THAT
MODIFIES YOUR VERB? *CONSTANTLY*

HERE'S YOUR POEM:
THE SNOW
  EVER-FALLING, BLINDING
ON WISCONSIN
  HEAVILY, CONSTANTLY
DROPPING.

(Quoted in Wresch, 1985, pp. 124–125)

In addition to making everybody an instant poet, *Compupoem* also offers to give advice on fourteen categories of poetry writing in general—from the uses of phrases and nouns, to Zen, to "making it strange."

In the case of *Compupoem*, primary socialization (i.e., the student's first real encounter with how to think about the nature of poetry) represents Roszak's worst fears about conditioning students to acquiesce to the banality of the programmmer's understanding of poetry while reinforcing the cultural orientation that upholds the superiority of technique over human imagination and insight. For readers who have themselves been socialized to think of poetry as merely the clever arrangement of words, it might be useful to compare Gary Snyder's view of the poet; his agreement with Ezra Pound's view of the artist as the antennae of humanity suggests a very different view of what is involved in poetic expression than the view imprinted on the student's mind by *Compupoem*.

According to Snyder, the poet has

> a sense of the need to look at the key archetype image and symbol blocks and sees if the blocks are working. Poetry effects change by fiddling with the archetypes and getting at people's dreams about a century before it actually effects historical change. A poet would be, in terms of the ecology of symbols, noting the main structural connections and seeing which parts of the symbol system are no longer useful or applicable, though everyone is giving them credence. . . . Poets are more like mushrooms or fungus—they can digest the symbol-detritus. (1980, p. 71)

It should be obvious that what students acquire as they interact with the computer program, casually choosing words and watching how a poem magically appears on the screen, is not depth of experience and the ability to recognize what is not seen by others. The technology, in a sense, falsifies achievement by substituting the conceptual formulas of the software program, which enables everybody to experience instant achievement, for the kind of insight that comes from working out the deeper meaning of our relationships within time (the past-present-future continuum) and space (our social and natural ecology). The cultural message students are more likely to acquire from *Compupoem* is that creativity is a form of impulse release; as long as the students' form of involvement contributes to a sense of fun, fits the conceptual norms dictated by the software program, and does not lead to questions that disrupt the timing sequence of the program or force the turning off of the machine in order to deal with them, it will be seen as educational.

An article by Robert Van Deusen and Jean Donham (1986–87) on using the microcomputer to teach thinking skills puts the problem facing teachers in proper perspective: "It is the teacher who teaches; the software is the medium" (p. 34). Unfortunately, the interpretation of the teacher's responsibilities either involves a technicist set of concerns (the long lists of procedures and strategies) or disappears into a deep silence that reflects the ideological orientation of the profession. It is now time to return to the question: What are the responsibilities of the teacher in relationship to the process of educational computing? Although we shall later use examples drawn from educational computing, the critical judgments teachers must be prepared to exercise as the process of primary socialization evolves also relate to the use of other modes of communication in the classroom, including the spoken and written word as well as the cultural messages embedded in nonverbal communication.

The educational moments when the student is learning something for the first time (which may include learning to think about how aspects of the culture have been integrated into experience at the tacit level; e.g., Douglas's observation about background knowledge) involve a dependency relation with the significant other (teacher, parent, peer, and so forth). How the dynamics of the process are controlled by the significant other (hereafter referred to as the teacher, although this is not always the case in some areas of primary socialization) will have a profound effect on whether the process contributes to the conceptual foundations necessary for further empowerment in communicative competence or limits the students in their ability to think and communicate by further embedding them in the prevailing recipe beliefs of the culture (Bowers, 1987a, b). That the latter may be appropriate in some instances further complicates how we view the teacher's professional responsibilities. It should be kept in mind that there are a number of additional variables and that we are identifying only the more critical ones that are under the teacher's immediate control. We shall use the metaphor of a langauge game to suggest that, like a chess game, changing the "moves" in the process of primary socialization changes the outcome of the educational process, particularly when the teacher understands the dynamics of the process. Even when teachers do not have this understanding, they will be caught up in primary socialization, but not in a manner that enables them to recognize how they contribute to empowerment or control. After we have identified the four essential "moves" in the language game of primary socialization, we shall return to the *Voyageur* program for the purpose of clarifying the professional judgments that teachers should make when the microcomputer is the mediating technology in the socialization process.

Control of the Language–Thought Connection

Learning something for the first time at an explicit level (e.g., how do we think about time, poetry, fur traders) involves a naming process. In some instances the teacher, as a gatekeeper, literally provides the words and concepts that will serve as the initial interpretative framework to guide the student's subsequent thought. In effect, the language (e.g., image and generative metaphors that frame thought and provide the conceptual building blocks, like the language students were given to think about "computer literacy") provides the initial conceptual schema for understanding. If the teacher provides a limited vocabulary and set of concepts, the student's initial ability to conceptualize and communicate about the newly acquired understandings will be limited—most likely in a manner that reflects the taken-for-granted beliefs of the teacher or the person who wrote the software program or textbook. The professional responsibility of the teacher is to be sensitive to whether the symbolic tools (words, concepts for understanding relationships) made available to students are adequate for understanding the complexity of the cultural experience under discussion. The teacher's own taken-for-granted beliefs will be a powerful influence on the language code that is made available in this critical moment in which the first words in the naming process play such a formative role in the development of the student's thought. In effect, the teacher's own past socialization will influence whether the gatekeeper role over the student's access to the symbolic resources of the culture will be a facilitating one. Regardless of teachers' levels of awareness, they will exercise control over the language code during the most critical phase of socialization—which is not to argue that students will not come under the influence of other "significant others" or bring aspects of their own understanding to bear on what they are being told.

Making Explicit the Taken-for-Granted Beliefs

Primary socialization also involves the teacher's communicating a natural attitude (primarily through nonverbal communication) toward the explanations that are being shared with students. Again, many variables enter into the ecology of relationships, but a taken-for-granted attitude toward a highly simplistic and generally nonproblematic explanation will, for many students who are hearing something for the first time, lead them to adopt the same taken-for-granted attitude. Depending upon the conceptual orientation of the teacher, this may vary from sharing a sense of the natural order of the social world to questioning and treating explanations as somebody's interpretation. This aspect of primary socialization is the most difficult to deal with, since teachers must first become aware of their own taken-for-granted beliefs before they can be aware of them in textbooks and instructional software. The failure of teachers to recognize sexist language until the issue was politicized in the larger social arena serves as a powerful reminder of how difficult it is to be aware of the taken-for-granted beliefs that are "regarded as too true to warrant discussion"—to again quote Mary Douglas.

Control over the "Objectification" of the Message

A third element of primary socialization, which occurs simultaneously with providing the conceptual scaffolding of thought and modeling a natural attitude toward what is being shared, involves another critically important choice for teachers. This has to do with whether the teacher leaves students with the impression that an explanation is purely factual and objective or instead espouses a more historical perspective that encourages students to consider the origins of the ideas under consideration; the latter requires a more complex language code, which the teacher controls. If students encounter an explanation through the textbook, software program, or teacher that suggests objectivity, factualness, and universal truth (characteristics of digital knowledge), then the dynamics of the socialization process are being used in a manner that will limit the student's conceptual development. On the other hand, if the teacher encourages a more historical perspective, students will acquire the conceptual foundation for critical judgment. It is important to recognize here that a historical perspective will not automatically lead students to reject what they are being presented; instead they are more likely to understand that what represented an intelligent response to a past situation may today be in need of revision. Students may also develop a clearer understanding that knowledge is related to interests and power relationships and that it reflects the assumptions of a historically situated conceptual framework.

Control over the Generative Metaphors

Primary socialization involves the interplay of the explicit explanation with a conceptual framework of background assumptions that provide a sense of conceptual coherence of the part and the whole. When first-grade teachers explain how to "tell" time, they generally reinforce the background cultural assumptions about time being linear, measurable, and so forth. Similarly, explanations about technology are generally embedded in the background assumptions about progress, success, and an anthropocentric universe. The professional judgment that teachers must be able to exercise has to do with recognizing when the explanations are based on background assumptions that no longer make sense or, worse, may contribute to the ecological and cultural crisis we now face. The background assumptions, often expressed in the form of a generative metaphor, must then be made explicit and understood in terms of their historical development.

CLARIFYING CULTURAL ASSUMPTIONS

The use of simulation, data-base, and drill and practice programs either constitutes primary socialization or reinforces cultural patterns of thought learned elsewhere. When microcomputers are utilized in the classroom, the teacher has the same professional responsibilities as when other technologies are used; namely, to control the dynamics of the socialization process in a manner that contributes to students' ability to put their own cultural experiences into perspective and to address in a meaningful way the adequacy of the conceptual and moral foundations of the modern world. This is the area in which teachers have a primary responsibility; it is also the basis of their authority. Carrying out this responsibility can be facilitated by a knowledge of the technical functions of the microcomputer, but it is not dependent upon being "computer literate." On the other hand, knowing how to program the computer or to use various software programs does not in itself contribute to the teacher's ability to understand, within the context of a lesson, the interaction of language and thought or the equally complex interplay of foreground (explicit) and background (implicit) knowledge. Nor do the guidelines on how to foster thinking skills, as this is presently understood, help teachers understand the appropriateness of a generative metaphor for framing the thought process or the danger of reinforcing current misconceptions about individualism and the neutrality of language.

We shall use the *Voyageur* program (see Figure 4.1) as an example to demonstrate the importance of an awareness of the process of primary socialization as the basis for the exercise of a distinct set of professional judgments. Although the purpose of the simulation is to teach decision making within the framework of a limited and known set of options, the use of a fur-trading expedition as the context for the simulation involves primary socialization in how to understand the early experiences of the fur traders and indigenous peoples. It also involves further reinforcement of a number of cultural assumptions that most students in the dominant culture will have already encountered—such as the materialistic view of success; the separation of culture and nature, with the latter viewed as a "hostile" environment; and the notion of the autonomous individual. The identification of how teachers can supplement the use of this software program in order to prevent primary socialization from becoming a highly restrictive process of passing on outworn cultural beliefs should be viewed as equally pertinent to the use of other instructional software programs. The example will also serve to illuminate how the teacher orchestrates the moves in the language game of primary socialization.

The conceptual scaffolding for how students will think about life in the woods of northern Minnesota in the eighteenth century is established by the language the program makes available on the monitor. In addition to the reference to the territory as "Northern Minnesota" (what was it called by the indigenous peoples?), the students will read that "fur trading was the main industry" in this part of the "unsettled wilderness." The students will also read that they are to think of themselves as working for the John Jacob Astor Fur Trading Company and that their goal is to reach "Rainy Lake in the least

Figure 4.1 Segments from the *Voyageur* simulation program

Screen 1

INTRODUCTION

This program is a simulation of the early 18th century in the woods of Northern Minnesota.

Fur trading was the main industry at this time. During this period, Minnesota was still part of the unsettled wilderness.

You are a fur trader working for the American Fur Company under John Jacob Astor.

Your goal is to reach Rainy Lake in the least amount of time with the most furs.

(Press space bar to continue)

Screen 2

DAY 3
OUTARDE PORTAGE

Indians sighted

You have 2 pieces to trade with.

Do you want to trade with them?

Screen 3

DAY 3
OUTARDE PORTAGE

You have 2 pieces to trade.

They have:		
	Beaver	19
	Fox	10
	Muskrat	17
	Wolf	12
	Total	58

How much do you want to give them?

Indians accept

You get the furs and they should get 1 piece.

(Press space bar to continue)

Source: Kinzer, Sherwood, and Brandsford, 1986, p. 275

amount of time with the most furs." If we can put aside the decisions that must be made to achieve this goal—decisions about clothes, gunpowder, food supplies, and so forth—and consider the educational rather than the play aspects of the simulation, we can put in focus the teacher's responsibility for supplementing the students' encounter with the mind of the people who created the software program.

The initial and most controlling phase of primary socialization is where significant others, the software program in this case, provide the language that is to serve as the basis for subsequent thought. In the case of *Voyageur* the language propels to the foreground a limited understanding of the actual situation: terms such as *Northern Minnesota, industry,* and *unsettled wilderness* will lead most students to project onto this period their own assumptions about what these terms mean. Secondly, the limited language weakens the students' ability to recognize or articulate the characteristics of the existing cultural ecology—the people who lived there, their social practices and belief systems, their way of using the energy and food resources of the region. This was not an "unsettled wilderness," nor were the fur traders simply driven by the desire to get the most furs in the least amount of time. They were, in fact, complex individuals who were less conditioned by their cultural traditions than the people who wrote the *Voyageur* program. They often lived with the indigenous peoples and adopted many of their cultural practices. As carriers of an alien cultural tradition, they had to be skilled in adjusting cultural expectations to different contexts.

Changing the dynamics of primary socialization requires that the teacher give attention to whether the students are given the language that provides the basis for thinking about the complexity of the situation being described. This also involves helping students recognize the metaphorical nature of language; that is, what a word or phrase means to the student and program writer (e.g., *time, work, wilderness*) may have had an entirely different meaning to the people being studied. To put it another way, the teacher needs to be alert to whether a conduit view of language has been written into the program. If it has, students will be further conditioned (reinforced) to accept the cultural myth of objective knowledge and to project onto others their own cultural assumptions.

Attention to the content of the program—the metaphorical language and embedded cultural assumptions—lead automatically to the other aspects of primary socialization. Our brief examination of how the language made available in the *Voyageur* program frames the students' understanding touches on the taken-for-granted beliefs of the authors of the program. Making explicit the cultural assumptions embedded in the program, as well as the assumptions of the people being studied, requires an alert teacher who is both sensitive and skillful in helping students put in perspective taken-for-granted assumptions that otherwise would go unnoticed. The taken-for-granted assumptions embedded in the *Voyageur* program include the Western proclivity to view success in economic terms, the indigenous people as not having a developed culture (thus the reference to "wilderness"), the individual as autonomous and self-directing, and the land as needing to be exploited.

In order for the teacher to put these cultural assumptions in perspective, the other "moves" in the language game of primary socialization must be changed. The identification of taken-for-granted beliefs leads to the pedagogically significant question of where the beliefs came from. Asking about the origin of beliefs and values introduces students to thinking about the continuities between the present and past. This can lead to understanding how the assumptions of the past are re-enacted as part of the natural attitude toward the present. It can also lead to an examination of the cultural forces that contributed to a particular way of thinking; for example, what cultural developments led to the view of time (as equated with efficiency) that is contained in *Voyageur* program? Also, what were the origins of the assumption that separates the individual from the environment, thus allowing for the exploitation of the environment without diminishing the person who does the exploiting?

These are indeed difficult questions, and the introduction of a cross-cultural perspective is often the best (and easiest) way of addressing them. In terms of *Voyageur*, the teacher could provide the conceptual building blocks necessary for thinking about the deep cultural assumptions that organize experience into its distinct patterns by examining the beliefs and values that made up the symbolic templates of the indigenous cultures. For example, the following statement by Tatanka Yotanka in 1877 could provide a basis for an introductory comparison between the conceptual underpinnings of the indigenous cultures and that of the European fur traders and early settlers: "Every seed is awakened and so has all animal life. It is through this mysterious power that we too have our being and we therefore yield to our neighbors, even our animal neighbors, the same right as ourselves, to inhabit this land" (quoted in McLuhan, 1971, p. 90). This statement about essential relationships stands in sharp contrast to the cultural assumptions that underlie the decision-making process students will simulate as they attempt to complete the journey in the most efficient and profitable way.

THE POLITICS OF TEACHING

It would be useful here to relate primary socialization to the point made by Martin Fischler and Oscar Firschein, two researchers in artificial intelligence who adopt a view that is very close to the sociology-of-knowledge position:

> An observed phenomenon is interpreted in accordance with a stored framework (model, metaphor, representation) that is used by a person to deal with the outside world. Different areas of human intellectual and emotional activities access different representations of the world with different attributes—they construct different realities. (1986, p. 44)

Although Fischler and Firschein ignore the role that language and culture play in the formation of the individual's interpretative framework, particularly the way in which "language speaks us," to quote Heidegger, their way of representing understanding as mediated by the socially acquired model or conceptual map (interpretive framework) helps clarify the nature of the teacher's control over the "mapmaking" process of primary socialization. If teachers adopt the stance that their role is to help students with procedural problems connected with running the software program or to teach students thinking skills ("hypothesis testing," "inductive reasoning," and so forth), the students are likely to acquire as part of their interpretive framework all the cultural assumptions and conceptual patterns that are taken for granted by the person who created the software program. The *Voyageur* program is an excellent example of how a concern with teaching thinking skills obscures the more important educational issue—namely, how the cultural content of the program contributes to the development of an interpretive framework that will lead to a distorted way of understanding historical events and weaken the ability to understand self as a cultural being.

By emphasizing the teacher's responsibility to monitor the cultural content of the program (the framing characteristics of language, taken-for-granted assumptions, the false sense of objectivity, and the reinforcement of the generative metaphors—master conceptual templates that underlie the cultural view of reality), we are suggesting that educational computing does not change the teacher's responsibility for providing the symbolic foundation necessary for an informed and critically reflective form of thought. When the teacher's responsibility is framed in this manner, it becomes obvious that cultural literacy (that is, the ability to decode the taken-for-granted nature of cultural patterns), rather than a view of computer literacy that emphasizes procedural knowledge in the use of the machine and software program, is the key problem that needs to be addressed.

As the recent awareness of gender-specific versus gender-neutral language has shown, the process of socialization is inherently political in nature. The exercise of power and control, the usual ingredients of politics, involves the way in which language helps create the conceptual framework that serves as the basis of the individual's understanding of relationships, ability to imagine alternative possibilities, and capacity for conceptually representing "what is." The teacher's control over how to represent the collective cultural experience through metaphorical language is part of this political process. Contrary to current belief, educational computing is also part of the political process of conceptual mapmaking. As explained earlier, the emphasis on manipulating data as the source of empowerment grows out of the liberal ideological tradition that views change as progressive, locates authority within the reflective judgment of the individual, and gives observation and measurement a privileged status as the foundation of knowledge. This ideological orientation, which continues to serve as a source of legitimation for continued technological development, also underlies the capitalist social order. Although capitalism has contributed to the creation of material well-being for many and significant opportunities for self-expression, its emphasis on profits and the use of rationality to maximize efficiency has also undermined the moral basis of responsibility between individual persons and between individuals and the environment. In effect, this liberal tradition is the master idea that frames (makes sensible) the current reduction of experience to data and promises power and wealth to those who possess the technical ability to store and manipulate data.

Given the inherently political nature of primary socialization (whether it is consciously guided or not) and the ideological orientation that has shaped the development of computer technology, we need to return to the question of which values should guide the teacher's involvement in the process of primary socialization. That we are a pluralistic culture, involving different and often conflicting conceptual maps, makes the possibility of a consensus especially elusive. Unfortunately, the teacher's political involvement in influencing the conceptual foundations of the student's thought cannot wait until a unified set of values is worked out. The choice of instructional software, the subtle directing of a classroom discussion, and the sharing of taken-for-granted beliefs will each have an influence on the makeup of the student's symbolic world. Just as traditional gender distinctions were maintained through the use of a language code that teachers took for granted, student attitudes toward community, environment, and existential purpose are influenced by a different set of the cultural prejudices transmitted through the spoken and written word, as well as by the areas of silence in the curriculum where the vocabulary and conceptual categories essential for translating experience into thought are withheld.

As contending individual and group voices are raised, thus adding confusion rather than a clear sense of direction about our guiding social values, teachers must continue to make curricular decisions. This includes decisions about the use of instructional software programs, as well as about the attitudes that are to be taught concerning the place technology should have in our lives. In this period of uncertainty about our guiding values, it seems that two basic questions could serve as reference points for evaluating the process of primary socialization in the classroom. The questions of *how to live* and *where to live* point to the importance of reconstituting the moral foundations of our relationships in the modern world and of insuring that social practices do not destroy the habitat upon which we are so utterly dependent. These two questions cannot be answered from a partisan perspective, because the answers of any one social group will be seen as an imposition by others who ground their sense of authority in their own historically distinct set of experiences and collective mythology. Nor can the questions be answered through technological advances in the processing of data. The problems of how to live and where to live are linked to the breakdown of the master ideas that served, albeit imperfectly, as the moral and conceptual compass that provided past generations a coherent and compelling sense of direction. Although we cannot embrace the master ideas of the past as a totally reliable guide in the modern world (in fact, many of these master ideas are responsible for crises we are now experiencing), the need to reconstitute shared master ideas suggests that schools have a distinct responsibility that is not likely to be carried out by other institutions. The responsibility is to insure that in the ongoing processes of primary socialization students have the opportunity to consider the symbolic foundations of their own cultural traditions, as well as those of other cultural groups who have worked out viable answers (a form of analogic knowledge) to the questions of how to live with each other in a morally responsible way and how to live in harmony with the environment. The oral and literate traditions—poems, personal narratives, epic stories, allegories, folk stories, teachings of prophets and artisans—are an important source of analogic knowledge about how to live with each other (including the nonhuman members of the bio community). A knowledge of the history of ideas, institutions, and social practices is also part of the symbolic world that needs to be recovered as part of formal education.

The recovery of the symbolic foundations of thought is not a distinct and esoteric activity for teachers. As they incorporate into the process of primary socialization the historical and (when appropriate) cross-cultural perspectives, as well as insure that the explanatory power of the language is tested against the experience of the entire community, they are contributing to the students' symbolic resources. This is part of the empowerment process. But beyond this, an awareness of the two basic questions relating to how and where to live leads to a greater sensitivity to whether the content of the curriculum—textbooks, instructional software, social practices in the classroom—contributes to a cultural orientation that emphasizes achievement over the quality of relationships, change over a concern with excellence and meaningful order, and power to manipulate the environment over development of the inner self.

In a very real sense, the adaptation of the microcomputer for classroom use has not really altered the fundamentals of good teaching. The teacher's moral and intellectual responsibility is to keep alive what Robert Bellah and colleagues call the "community of memory." Since we tend to think of community in a very superficial manner, it would be useful to quote their fuller understanding of a moral ecology:

> Communities, in the sense in which we are using the term, have a history—in an important sense they are constituted by their past—and for this reason we can speak of a real community as a "community of memory," one that does not forget its past. In order not to forget that past, a community is involved in retelling its story, its constitutive narrative, and in so doing, it offers examples of the men and women who have embodied and exemplified the meaning of the community. These stories of collective history and exemplary individuals are an important part of the tradition that is so central to a community of memory.
>
> The stories that make up a tradition contain conceptions of character, of what a good person is like, and of the virtues that define such character. But the stories are not all exemplary, not all about successes and achievements. A genuine community of memory will also tell painful stories of shared suffering that sometimes creates deeper identities than success. . . . And if the community is completely honest, it will remember stories not only of suffering received but of suffering inflicted—dangerous memories, for they call the community to alter ancient

> evils. The communities of memory that tie us to the past also turn us toward the future as communities of hope. They carry a context of meaning that can allow us to connect our aspirations for ourselves and those closest to us with the aspirations of a larger whole and see our own efforts as being, in part, contributions to a common good. (1985, p. 153)

This approach to thinking about the community of memory needs to be extended backward in time by taking seriously the cultural experience of the oral tradition, as well as broadened to include the nonhuman forms of life that, as Gary Snyder (1980) observes, are the sources of energy that flow into our lives.

Reconstituting the symbolic foundations of the community of memory, as part of the formal educational experiences of youth, would help put in proper perspective the importance of data, procedural thinking, and the sense of power that is associated with computer technology. It would also help to keep in focus the importance of teachers' understanding their responsibilities for guiding the process of primary socialization, regardless of whether a book or an instructional software program is the chief technological resource. The myths of individualism and the neutrality of technology have led to an overemphasis on facts and data in the educational process, and thus on delivery systems that will connect students in the most direct and efficient manner to the experts who create the facts and data. The teacher's responsibility in the intellectual process, which is the essence of primary socialization when it is carried out in a more empowering manner, has been correspondingly de-emphasized to the point where many teachers, like the one quoted early in this chapter who viewed educational computing as a threat, are uncertain about their role. Until teachers reclaim their moral and intellectual responsibilities to students, and educational-computing experts recognize that the nontechnical educational issues are the primary ones yet to be addressed, it is likely that the educational use of computers will be driven by the forces of the marketplace and by the cultural myths that put out of focus what we are doing to ourselves and our environment.

CHAPTER 5

Educational Computing in Third World Countries: A Restatement of Themes

A geography book published in 1896, reflecting the cultural assumptions of the day, made the point that the cultures of the world could be situated in one of three categories, and that these categories represented distinct stages in the evolutionary development of cultures. The key for determining whether a culture was to be placed in the category of "savage or uncivilized," "half-civilized," or "civilized" was the degree to which literacy had been adopted. Uncivilized people "know nothing about reading or writing and spend much of their time in hunting and fishing" (*Eclectic Elementary Geography*, 1896, p. 15). The civilized cultures, on the other hand, were Western and had adopted an institutionalized approach to literacy. The language has changed in that *uncivilized* and *half-civilized* are now politically and morally unacceptable words. Yet the underlying belief in a linear, progressive process of cultural development has been retained, with evolutionary development now viewed in terms of a traditional culture's becoming modern (including the adoption of the form of thinking that underlies Western science and technology). The institutionalization of literacy (schools) is still an important criterion for being considered modern. Now, however, modernization also means the integration of computers into the educational and economic infrastructure of society. With the growing tendency to equate modernization with the Information Age and the computer technology that makes information processing possible on a massive scale, the old notion of literacy is being updated. Ironically, computer literacy, the phrase that is so problematic within our own cultural context, is becoming a new hallmark of modernization and thus the goal to be achieved by Third World countries who do not wish to be viewed as culturally backward (Mazrui, 1978).

Computer literacy is being promoted by a wide range of educational spokespersons and international agencies as a goal of schools in Third World countries. Computer manufacturers such as IBM give impetus to this movement by donating computers to these countries and helping educate people in how to use them. UNESCO and other agencies of the United Nations have given special legitimacy to computer literacy by funding major projects designed to encourage the spread of computer use. Jean-Jacques Servan-Schreibner, former president of the Paris-based World Center for Microcomputer and Human Resources, summarized the rationale for this push for computer literacy in terms that equate the development of computer technology with the fullest realization of human and cultural potential.

> The computer revolution is the first intellectual revolution in 500 years. It is bound to transform every aspect of the human endeavor—agriculture, industry, the office, medicine, education. To ignore this revolution is to make oneself irrelevant. . . . Every characteristic—creativity, imagination, talent—that makes a human being different from a machine can be enhanced by the computer revolution. . . . [With regard to education,] when computer and telecommunications networks are sufficiently developed, the lectures, research, and new findings of important intellectuals and academics can be made available to students around the world. (quoted in Branfman, 1985, p. 571)

This vision of the modernizing process, which has the appearance of transcending the political realm wherein the interests of one cultural group are favored over others, is also being promoted by educational leaders in Third World countries. In the West African republic of Senegal, for example, a director of a school who helped establish a computer laboratory in spite of exceedingly limited financial resources justifies the effort with the statement that "when there is a tool that can be used by mankind, we must do our best to master it. I am convinced that computers are one of these tools" (quoted in McCorduck, 1985, p. 183). The head of the research center of the École Normale Supérieure remarked to an American visitor that the computer, for the first time in the history of civilization, provides all societies a new and more equal starting point. The view that equates technology with the historical necessity of modernization is repeated in the explanation given by another Senegal educational leader who justifies educational computing this way:

> We must do this. To . . . teachers who worry that this is one piece of silly technology, we say no, that the language of computing teaches children to learn by themselves, creating their own tasks, solving their own problems. We also tell them that unlike books, unlike films and records, there is a degree of interactivity here that makes learning qualitatively different from anything else. (McCorduck, 1985, p. 188)

Two graduate students from Arab countries expressed to me somewhat different reasons for wanting to integrate computers into the educational systems of their respective countries. Although both were politically conscious individuals, they shared the view that computer technology is culturally neutral. In one case the reason given for wanting to introduce educational computing was that it would help reduce the percentage of non-Saudi secondary teachers; in effect the computer was being viewed as a means of reducing the introduction of foreign beliefs and values. The second graduate student, who was both culturally and religiously conservative, was deeply concerned about the threat of cultural invasion from the West; for example, feminism, secularism, and individualism. Although he did not entirely accept the Western myth about the neutrality of technology, he was unable to articulate the connection between the cultural-amplification characteristics of educational computing and the intrusion of Western culture into his society. Both students were bright and highly educated individuals who are likely to assume leadership roles in the educational development of their respective countries, but like so many foreign students they have unconsciously acquired, through their exposure to Western education, the assumptions underlying science and technology—including the belief that technology can contribute to a nondependent form of social development.

If these views on the importance of educational computing had not been attributed to African and Arab educators, they could easily have been viewed as statements taken either from American educational-computing textbooks or made by our leading computer spokespersons. The similarity of views on how educational computing fits into the big picture of human progress is not difficult to explain. Key advocates of computer literacy in Third World countries have graduate degrees in educational computing from American universities. And if they are not acquiring the view that equates computer technology with modernization from us, they are learning it from their contacts with Canadian, British, French, and other Western universities where the myths of progress and the neutral nature of technology still survive.

In my own institution, for example, we have bright students from Latin America, Africa, Asia, and the Middle East who, following their study of educational computing, will return home to assume educational leadership positions within their own society. For them, learning how to use the computer and integrate it into the learning process of the classroom also involves acquiring a set of cultural assumptions that will, if accepted uncritically, serve as an interpretive framework for understanding that Western technology and science represents the most advanced stage in cultural evolution. Like much of primary socialization, these cultural assumptions—which are embedded in the dominant epistemology of the university community—are learned at a tacit level; that is, they are learned as part of the conceptual background that provides a framework for understanding the procedural aspects of educational computing. The criteria for determining what constitutes the most progressive stage of cultural development has changed substantially since 1896, but the ability of the West to control the definition of what constitutes progress (understood now in terms of modernization rather than in terms of the old "uncivilized"-"civilized" continuum) is still largely the same.

There is a certain element of irony in accepting a Western view of modernization and progress. The word *tragic,* in its original Greek sense, might even be a more appropriate term than *irony*. The acceptance of such seemingly bedrock truths that equate technological development with progress and accessibility of information with individual empowerment, as well as all the correlative assumptions about the culture-free nature of the rational process (including the scientific method), technology, and language, comes at a time when the assumptions underlying the dominant conceptual template we associate with modern consciousness are coming under critical scrutiny. The critical attitude that characterizes the debate within the West is not prompted simply by a failure of a cultural sense of self-confidence or a loss of the hubris that was a partial source of expansionist energy. Rather it is prompted by an awareness of fundamental discrepancies between the ideals that surround and legitimize the core Western beliefs and values and the worsening of social and environmental conditions. The continuing fascination with the steady stream of high-tech developments and the further mesmerism of an increasingly materialistically oriented consumerism serve to hide from many people the serious reconsideration of basic values that is now going on in Western societies. But the deterioration of the social fabric, which goes far beyond the loss of civic values and the disruption of the natural environment, has reached the point where the more thoughtful observer is being forced to reconsider the growing disjuncture between the vision associated with modernization and the realities of everyday life.

The foreign students studying educational computing, at least at my own university, do not usually come in contact with the ideas of Habermas, Nietzsche, Heidegger, and Foucault—the philosophers who have laid out the foundations for a critique of modern consciousness. Nor are they likely to have read Hannah Arendt, Wendell Berry, Robert Bellah, David Noble, Alasdair MacIntyre, Evelyn Fox Keller, and Theodore Roszak—who are representative of social theorists who have chosen to address more specific aspects of the crisis. The point is not whether foreign students have been exposed to the ideologically correct social critics, but whether they are exposed in their course work to *any* coherent conceptual framework that would provide for a critical understanding of the problematic aspects of modern consciousness. A more likely program of study would be a large number of educational-computing courses that seemingly explore every possible classroom application, from "computer spreadsheets for teachers" to "computers in composition." By the time the students have done additional work in learning theory (which does not take account of culture or the metaphorical nature of language), teaching strategies, and curriculum design, as well as taken a course or two in computer science, where they might learn the basics of a computer language, they will have completed the credit-hour requirement for a master's or perhaps even a doctoral degree. But in not being exposed to the conceptual frameworks that now inform the current debate on our guiding values and beliefs, they are likely to return home believing that at least Western technology and science are culturally neutral and can be used to modernize their own societies. Feminism, individualism, and the emporium of consumer choice that is spreading across our land, by way of contrast, are likely to evoke more ambiguous attitudes and thus not be seen as aspects of Western modernism that can be easily transferred to the classrooms of their own societies. But the case for introducing computer literacy in the schools will seem clear and compelling, demanding the promotion of educational computing to keep in step with the progressive movement of the modernizing process.

It is important to emphasize here that I am not arguing against the educational use of microcomputers in Third World countries or social development that is influenced by Western ideas and values. These are issues that must be decided by each cultural group. The concern being addressed here has to do with basing a decision about the introduction of educational computing on the assumption that technology is culturally neutral, adaptable to the local culture simply by changing the content of the instructional software program. Although Servan-Schreibner's statement about computers transforming "every aspect of the human endeavor" may turn out to be partially true, we have no way of knowing whether the transformation will, on the whole, be beneficial or harmful to humanity. He chooses to view only the positive benefits, ignoring the potential use (developed now to a considerable degree) of computer technology to increase the surveillance of citizens by the state or the likelihood of a nuclear war caused by a malfunction of the technology that is programmed to take over more of the human decision-making process. The critical point that his optimism, as well as that of the Senegalese official quoted earlier, puts out of focus is that the introduction of a technology, any technology, represents an experiment with the culture into which it is introduced. The consequences, in terms of changes in social patterns, values, and ways of thinking as well as the introduction of new traditions and the loss of old ones, cannot be known in advance. Only hindsight provides the perspective for making a meaningful judgment, and often it comes too late to reverse the process.

Another point that needs to be understood about the culturally experimental nature of technological innovation, particularly technologies that have not evolved out of indigenous traditions, is that when traditions are disrupted and cease to be part of the ongoing patterns of everyday life they cannot arbitrarily be recovered. To make this point is not to suggest that all traditions should be preserved. Rather, the problem is to insure, insofar as possible, that viable traditions are not lost because attention was diverted by a narrow understanding of the innovative technology. As Edward Shils observes, "Traditions are not independently self-reproductive or self-elaborating. Only living, knowing, desiring human beings can enact them and reenact them and modify them" (1981, pp. 14–15). When they are lost they cannot be recovered in living form; they will instead exist as empty rituals and externally prescribed patterns. On the other hand, technological innovations, such as the introduction of microcomputers into a Senegalese or Saudi classroom, may start new traditions. But whether they will survive or become integrated into existing patterns in a positive manner cannot be determined in advance.

With these warnings in mind about the culturally experimental nature of technological innovation and the nonrecoverable nature of living traditions, it is important to understand the wide range of policy issues that are being indirectly, and perhaps unconsciously, decided when a technology such as a microcomputer is introduced into a culture in order to facilitate progressive social development. Often the decisions will be made without being formally recognized as a policy issue, but the effect will be the same. In order to make the discussion more concrete we shall now turn to the selection, amplification, and reduction characteristics of technology that we discussed earlier. These mediating characteristics relate directly to policy issues that should be recognized and consciously dealt with before a technology such as educational computing is introduced into a non-Western culture. This discussion also relates to the problem of using microcomputers to teach children of indigenous cultures in North America their native language, as well as to the more general problem of misrepresenting the Information Age that we are educating all students to enter. But our focus will remain primarily upon educational computing in the Third World.

The questions raised by the use of microcomputers in Third World cultures cannot be reduced simply to whether to Westernize or not. Each culture involves so many variables in terms of traditions, patterns of thought and social practice, ways of framing experience, norms that guide sensory responses, and metaphorical images of self, that the use of a LOGO program, data base, or word processor will have a variable effect on each cultural ecology. In some cultures the use of a data base, which reinforces the importance of individual judgment, may involve the transmission of information traditionally regulated by ritual, gender, and age distinctions. That is, certain information might be shared only in certain ceremonial contexts and only by certain individuals who are seen as performing a unique responsibility. Depending on cultural context, the use of the individualistically oriented LOGO program might undermine the traditional image of self, the foundations of moral and intellectual authority, and the sense of what being in the world means. Given the range of differences in cultural patterns, it is impossible to approach the problem of borrowing the technology of another culture by analyzing the possible consequences for the new host cultural group. The problem must be framed in such a way that the culturally specific nature of the technology is made explicit; the responsibility for understanding the consequences of introducing this technology into a non-Western culture then rests, in part, on the borrower, who should be the best informed about local traditions and needs.

In *Understanding Computers and Cognition*, Terry Winograd and Fernando Flores go to the heart of the problem of the culturally specific view of the rational process that is built into existing computing technology, including educational software programs, by observing that a program represents the programmer's interpretation of the situation in which the program will function. But the assumptions about how the programmer approaches the problem of representing objects and relationship in the subject domain is based on views of the rational process, individualism, and the nature of language that are part of the Cartesian stream of Western philosophy. This is an important acknowledgment, as Winograd is himself an important figure within the field of artificial intelligence. Thus when he and Flores state that the symbols used by the programmer to represent a particular domain of experience always involve the use of "abstraction that produces blindness" (1986, p. 98) to certain aspects of the domain, their warnings must be taken seriously. They are not the concerned outsider like Roszak, whose contribution is in situating computer technology within the history of Western intellectual development, but insiders who recognize fully the unexamined epistemological assumptions that underlie the thinking of their colleagues in computing.

Winograd and Flores see two causes for not recognizing how a software program (that is, the information base of a problem-solving process) distorts what it purports to represent. The first, more general cause is the attempt to use an explicit language to represent the background, tacit domain of understanding. As they put it:

> The programmer acts within a context of language, culture, and previous understanding, both shared and personal. The program is forever limited to working within the world determined by the programmer's explicit articulation of possible objects, properties, and relations among them. It therefore embodies the blindness that goes with this articulation. (1986, p. 97)

The second cause of this conceptual blindness (or cultural bias), however, is rooted in the Cartesian view of the rational process that dominates the field of computing. This rationalistic tradition, according to Winograd and Flores, incorrectly views thinking as based in the mind's ability to objectify the external world, language as "a system of symbols that are composed into patterns that stand for things in the world," and cognition as individual-centered (1986, pp. 17–33).

One of the implications of language's reproducing a specific cultural orientation (in the case of computers, a specific tradition within Western thought) is that a language-based technology cannot be viewed as neutral. Thus the attempts by countries in Latin America, Africa, Asia, and the Middle East to encourage "computer literacy" by establishing centers and networks involve, at a deeper level, introducing into the modernization process of each country Western traditions of thought that made possible important advances in scientific understanding and more efficient technologies. But these advances, often represented as synonymous with modernization, have a negative side that has gone largely unnoticed; namely, the mode of thinking that underlies the Western approach to science and technology (including computing) undermines all forms of conceptual and moral authority except those that can be based on empirical evidence. As Roger Faber observes, the current scientific worldview is based on a mechanistic reduction of all living things (1986). When this mode of thought is extended into other areas of cultural life, it becomes nihilistic, undermining the traditional foundations of conceptual and moral authority that govern person-to-person and person-to-environment relationships. Although a strong case can be made that many traditional cultural practices are in need of revision, and even elimination, the nihilism (i.e., the relativizing of beliefs and values) spread by Western science and technology does not make a distinction between beneficial and malevolent, viable and outmoded traditions, displacing all by the new rationalistic form of authority. Theory building, collecting empirical evidence, efficiency in problem solving, and a conflict model of justification are the hallmarks of this modern scientific-technological form of consciousness that views cultural traditions and tacit knowledge as backward and unenlightened.

In writing about the computer as a modernizing technology, Ali Mazrui observes that modernization in Third World countries involves a shift in consciousness—from a concern with "custom and intuition to innovation and measurement," from a "preoccupation with ancestry and tradition to a concern for anticipation and planning, and from the holism of supernatural explanation to a concern with the temporal and specialized focus" (1978, p. 332). But to him modernization does not automatically translate into social, economic, and cultural development. "The computer in Africa," he acknowledges, "probably helps to promote modernization but it also aggravates Africa's technological and intellectual dependency on Western Europe and North America" (p. 332). While admitting that the more efficient use of the computer, and by extension, educational computing, would aid the process of planning, Mazrui warns that the consequences of computer use "are anti-developmental in such tasks as job creation, reducing dependency, conservation of foreign exchange, definition of priorities between town and country, and devising optimal salary structures for both locals and expatriates" (p. 340). As these are antidevelopmental consequences, the computer remains essentially paradoxical.

As suggested earlier, the cultural traditions of the host society, as well as the unique characteristics of the technology being borrowed, make it difficult to know in advance the consequence of cultural borrowing. But policy decisions at the local level can be informed by taking account of what is known about the distinctive characteristics of the technology—in terms of our interests, the educational use of the microcomputer. It is now time to restate these characteristics in order to see the broader policy issues that need to be addressed. That the four categories involve unavoidable overlap suggests the integrated character of the Western ideology (worldview) that is amplified through the educational use of the microcomputer.

THE CONDUIT VIEW OF LANGUAGE

Computer programs, according to Winograd and Flores, are based on a Western rationalistic tradition that incorporates a particular view about the nature of language. The model of language used includes the following assumptions:

> 1. Sentences in a natural language correspond to facts about the world.
> 2. It is possible to create a formal representation system such that:
>   (a) For any relevant fact about the world there can be a corresponding structure in the representation system.
>   (b) There is a systematic way of correlating sentences in natural language with structures in the representation system, so that the corresponding structure states the same fact as the sentence.
>   (c) Systematic formal operations on representation structures can be devised to carry out valid reasoning. (1986, p. 108)

The representations (that is, the "knowledge" that people have about the external world) are put into language and thus transferred to others. Computer programs, according to this view, are simply devices that store and manipulate the information or data that is "contained" in the language.

As Third World students enter (input) information into a data base or are the recipient of information programmed into simulation software, they will also be undergoing socialization to this conduit view of language. Language will appear to convey objective, decontextualized knowledge that is the basis for rational, individualistic judgment. In effect, socialization to a conduit view of language represents adopting one of the most basic aspects of the conceptual template that has had a privileged status in the West. The acceptance of objective knowledge (facts, data, information) as the basis of conceptual authority strengthens the possibility of social development proceeding along a Western social-political-cultural pathway. Instead of reinforcing traditional societal forms of authority (i.e., traditional practices and beliefs that have evolved over time, the personal authority of the speaker, authority associated with status position, and so forth), the new emphasis on objective knowledge will privilege the new social class of experts who possess the linguistic ability to collect and represent the meaning of the data at either a theoretical or mathematical level (i.e., statistics). As Alvin Gouldner notes, the diffuse precedents of traditional cultural practice, as well as the tacit features of conceptual and moral authority, will give way to the conceptual rules of a new class that will "authorize itself as the standard of *all* serious speech" (1979, pp. 28–29). An important characteristic of this new (and Western) model of thinking is that it is based on the assumption that out of a competitive (adversarial) intellectual process a more progressive understanding of truth and objectivity will emerge. In contrast to this approach, which Robin Horton (1982) refers to as "cognitive modernism," is the consensual mode of thinking that characterizes more traditional societies.

Basing decisions on objective information may strengthen other aspects of the modernizing process that are becoming both more prominent and more troubling: the strengthening of the role of the state, and thus the size of a bureaucracy that will have responsibility for collecting data on more aspects of social life; the use of theory as the basis of social planning, and thus the adoption of a more experimental attitude toward social development; and the politicizing of more areas of the person's lifeworld as tacit knowledge and traditional practices are organized on a more rationalistic basis. But a key to the modernizing process, as well as the particular direction it will take within any given culture, is the expansion of the capacity to obtain and store information (Giddens, 1981, p. 94). The centralization of the capacity to control knowledge within the apparatus of the state could undermine the importance of local knowledge and personal memory. Whether the spread of computer literacy, which could be enhanced by greater use of computers in the classroom, would foster centralization of political power and thus the loss of local forms of authority in maintaining cultural traditions is a point of current debate (see Mazrui, 1978). Some observers argue that computer literacy fosters the decentralizing of political power, since each person acquires a greater capacity to "access" the objective information necessary for independent judgment. But the decentralization of political power may be more a matter of appearance than substance if the use of the computer leads to the adoption of the same mind-set of the technocrats who represent the interests of the state.

DIGITAL VS. ANALOGUE KNOWLEDGE

When a technology like educational computing is represented as culturally neutral, while at the same time associated with modernization and progress, the deeper issues associated with changing the pathway of a culture become difficult to recognize. The distinction between analogue and digital knowledge may serve, in this situation, to illuminate another area of policy decision that needs to be given serious attention.

The borrowing of technology should involve a careful assessment of the original host culture. In the case of educational computing this would involve a careful assessment of the claims made on behalf of the technology, the purposes for which it is being used, the social groups who promote and benefit from its adoption, and the changes that it precipitates in the experience of work, social relationships, and guiding values and beliefs. An example of how technology reflects the mind-set and special interests of a particular social group can be seen in the argument that educational computing empowers people for living in the Information Age. This new age, so the argument goes, is witnessing the merging of North America, Europe, Japan, Australia, and other equally progressive countries into a mass communication network—a global village that is made more harmonious and productive through the sharing of information.

Thus the new prescription for achieving the status of a modern culture is to adopt the view that information is the source of empowerment—in business, politics, and social relationships. To put it in a manner that highlights the educational-policy issue that may be unconsciously decided by the desire to possess the technology accepted as the universal symbol of modernization: the adoption of educational computing will foster the digital form of knowledge that is to be exchanged through the information networks that link together modern cultures.

As educators in Third World countries consider the educational uses of the microcomputer, they need to think deeply about the claim that the Information Age represents the next stage in evolutionary process. Although it cannot be denied that, especially in Westernized cultures, massive amounts of information are being accumulated, there is still a question about whether the digital form of knowledge associated with information will become (or should become) the basis of our cognitive and moral authority. Perhaps the ideal of the Information Age, which is itself an interesting example of metaphorical thinking, is simply a powerful image used to represent the economic and political interests of people who gain from the creation and processing of more information.

At another level, one can ask whether a culture can turn its back on the analogue knowledge that is the basis of its traditions. If the analogue knowledge is not adequately communicated, it may become too attenuated to serve as a guide to human experience or provide the basis for updating these guiding patterns. Analogue knowledge, it must be emphasized, arises from the realm of human relationships; digital knowledge, as now constituted, is modeled upon a mechanistic way of thinking. Analogue knowledge is communal, whereas digital knowledge is atomistic. There is another basic distinction that is brought out in Papert's statement that "when knowledge can be broken up into 'mind-size bites,' it is more communicable, more assimilable, more simply constructable" (1980, p. 171). Whereas analogue knowledge is part of the ground of memory, and thus a source of a person's authority, digital knowledge involves the assumption that individuals possess the rational ability to use discrete bits of information to create ("building up" in Papert's words) new patterns and technologies. Memory, and the power of perspective that it gives, is not as important as the ability to process more data.

Roszak's point that we think with master ideas, and that they serve to give meaning, moral significance, and provide the templates for the instrumental use of information, should be kept in mind when considering the consequences of introducing educational computing into the curriculum. But the consideration of the importance of these master ideas, and how they are to be presented as part of the curriculum, should be separated from the Western myth of evolutionary development wherein modernization is equated with the highest stage of human development. The observation of Jean-Pierre Dupuy is critical to thinking against the grain of this deeply embedded myth.

> Rather than delivering us from material constraints, the informational society intensifies the struggle for survival and strengthens the radical monopoly of economic activity over the social and political dimensions of our life. We have grown accustomed to thinking of archaic or traditional societies as "subsistence economies," presuming that they exhaust

> themselves in organizing survival. Marshall Sahlins has enlightened us on this point: these societies do not dedicate more than three or four hours a day to material necessities. [By way of contrast] the only society in fact in which the struggle for survival absorbs the better part of our energies and intellect, occupying all available time and space, is industrial society. Instead of fostering harmony among people, then, the technologies of communication are aggravating alienation, producing a highly unstable, potentially explosive system. (1980, p. 5)

As others have echoed this view of modernization, it is important to avoid rejecting the master ideas simply because they are ancient, and not modern.

ORALITY AND LITERACY

Decisions about whether master ideas should be included in the school curriculum are critical to the "community of memory" that will provide a collective compass for charting the course of social development. It is important to consider whether these master ideas are dictated by the government or are derived from local knowledge tested over generations. The former are likely to be transmitted through print, while the spoken word is the chief means of transmitting the moral and conceptual templates that have cultural validity at the local level. This is not to suggest that only books contain knowledge that represents the interests of governments or that local and national interests never coincide. Rather the distinction being made here is a more subtle one. Since literacy appears to be an essential, thus an inevitable, aspect of social development, an important question about the content of the school curriculum relates to whose interests are served by the master ideas presented through the printed word. The balance that should be maintained between the local knowledge transmitted through the spoken word and the more universalizing perspective acquired through the written word should also be considered. Writing from the African perspective, Ali Mazrui states the problem with more force: "The nationalist task consists in indigenizing what is imputed and giving it greater consequence with the realities of its environment. But indigenizing the educational institution of Africa is in some ways more straightforward than re-rationalizing them." Referring more directly to the orality-literacy distinction (the latter being identified with Western rationalism), Mazrui notes

> The call for derationalization, from a nationalist point of view, is a call for national survival. A wave of modern research interest in African oral tradition and oral history is one step away from the rigid rationalism which has equated historical knowledge with written documentation bearing specific dates. (1978, pp. 210–12)

The implications for cultural invasion of using the school curriculum to privilege the printed word (literacy) over the spoken word (orality) can be seen in the functions performed by these two different forms of communication. In summarizing basic differences between print and voice, Ron and Suzanne Scollon observe that in the use of print the abstract "word comes to take precedence over the situation, analysis takes precedence over participation, isolated thought takes precedence over conversation and storytelling, and the individual takes precedence over the community" (1985, p. 10). In addition to the other cultural amplification characteristics of print—such as the fixed nature of the text that provides a basis for critical analysis, the individualizing and isolating nature of writing and reading, and the asymmetrical power relationship between the sender (writer) and receiver (reader)—there is another basic distinction that has emerged from recent attempts to understand, within the context of Western consciousness, the dominating role that the masculine view of reality has played.

Walter Ong, in his early studies of the difference between literacy and orality, noted that the former strengthens sight as the source of knowledge. Metaphorically, knowledge became associated with "illumination," "enlightenment," and "seeing the light," metaphors that reflect a Western view of knowledge. As *knowing* and *seeing* became synonymous terms, speaking and listening were accorded a lesser status. According to Western feminist writers, the association of seeing with hard facts and objective knowledge reflects a gender bias perpetuated by philosophers and scientists who were part of a patriarchal tradition. The particular form of masculinity that developed in the West led to a view of reality in which knowing was understood in terms of "mastering," "conquering," and the exercise of power over nature. Francis Bacon, an early contributor to this masculine interpretation of knowledge (which echoes the traditional view of the groom conquering the bride), was less circumspect than would be allowed today: "I am come in very truth" he wrote, "leading you to Nature with all her children to bind her to your service and make her your slave" (quoted in Keller, 1985, p. 79). This sense of visual separation between knower and known (subject and object) that yields objective knowledge about a passive external reality (nature, the Other) led, according to feminist critics, to relegating the other senses to an inferior status. Unlike the visual metaphors associated with the "discovery" of knowledge, voice metaphors suggest subjectivity and feminine weakness.

To bring the discussion back to the point made by the Scollons, the importance of the connection between the masculine model of knowing and the distancing gaze that contributes both to technological forms of power over nature and personal alienation from it can be seen by comparing the forms of relationships that are amplified by voice. As noted by the authors of *Women's Way of Knowing*, "unlike the eye, the ear operates by registering nearby subtle change. Unlike the eye, the ear requires closeness between subject and object. Unlike seeing, speaking and listening suggest dialogue and interaction" (Belenky, Clinchy, Goldberger, and Tarule, 1986, p. 18). The attempt on the part of feminist writers to recover voice as a legitimate source of knowledge—along with the values of caring and nurturing relationships, which are essential to both dialogue and the well-being of a larger sense of community—takes us back to the basic distinctions between orality and literacy. These distinctions, in turn, relate to policy issues that must be decided by educational leaders in Third World countries.

The social consequences of the narrative form of knowledge, which Jean-François Lyotard views as strengthening the conceptual and social skills that bond people together in community—"knowing how," "knowing how to speak," and "knowing how to hear" (1984, p. 21)—suggests the importance of incorporating oral traditions into the curriculum. This would insure that schools do not simply become conduits for transmitting decontextualized information (via textbooks and microcomputers) from an outside and more modern world. Knowledge acquired through speaking and listening means, as the Scollons point out, valuing participation over objective analysis and community over the isolated individual.

There is yet another reason for balancing literacy with orality. The ecological crisis is rooted, in part, in a mind-set that represents the individual as autonomous and the rational process as the chief means of mastering nature. Both aspects of this mind-set contribute to de-emphasizing the importance of relating understanding to context; this mind-set also devalues relational forms of knowledge. In correctly viewing alienation as an important aspect of the ecological crisis, the Scollons urge a fourfold set of concerns that can be met through a curriculum in which local knowledge is shared through the oral tradition.

But there is also a need for the more theoretical and scientific-based knowledge associated with literacy, knowledge that will enable the young to reconsider the misconceptions of the past. The fourfold educational agenda thus requires both forms of knowledge to foster learning about the basic categories of human existence that are common to all cultural groups: learning about one's place, learning about one's past, cultivating relationships, and enlarging the future.

According to the Scollons, learning about place involves acquiring an understanding of the soils, plants, and animal life of one's region; it also involves learning how economic practices and political decisions have affected the resource base of the bioregion. Learning about the past provides a basis for understanding how cultural traditions evolved in response to, as well as changed, the characteristics of the bioregion. This knowledge provides the basis for commitment to meaningful continuities, as well as the informed perspective required for modifying traditions that are no longer appropriate. The knowledge of past is basic to a sense of self and communal identity that encompasses relationships in the broadest sense, which is the third aspect of the Scollons' view of the educated person. Cultivating relationships involves learning to listen, to speak, to cooperate, and to be open to the new understandings that arise from these relationships. Knowledge of place and past contribute to a deeper understanding of relationships within the ecosystem. Lastly, enlarging the future, as opposed to the planning that characterizes the technological mindset, involves strengthening the sense of commitment to the future of the community and the bioregion; it involves strengthening decision-making processes at the local level and not viewing the implementation of outside technological solutions as necessarily the best way to solve local problems (Scollon & Scollon, 1985, pp. 33–35).

These educational concerns are not addressed in a curriculum whose textbooks and instructional software programs are written by Western experts or through instruction carried on in a language that is not native to the students. The objective knowledge that is to empower autonomous, rational decision making associated with the Western approach to education usually involves a view of language that emphasizes learning the content transmitted through the "conduit" of the printed word. The other view of language, which emphasizes relationships as the basis of significant message exchanges (communal knowledge), involves both the sharing of knowledge and a sensitivity to relationships. This latter view, now being highlighted in both the feminist and ecological literature, represents a challenge to the decontextualized knowledge associated with textbooks and instructional software programs.

COMPUTER LITERACY FOR TEACHERS IN THIRD WORLD COUNTRIES

Perhaps one of the most critically important issues in need of consideration is the education of the teachers and specialists who will guide the classroom use of microcomputers as well as influence, through their articulation of issues, how technology will be viewed. The efforts by such countries as India and Kuwait to adapt Western instructional software to the local culture by rewriting it in the native language are important. But changing the language in which the software is written, and adjusting content and presentation to conform to endogenous traditions, will not change the essential characteristics of this Cartesian technology. Regardless of the language in which the software is written, the microcomputer will mediate the transmission of culture. This will occur as the culturally specific view of rationality, individualism, and language (in this case, the Western Cartesian view) that underlies the development of the technology influences the aspects of culture that are selected and amplified, including the aspects of culture that cannot be represented. As suggested earlier, the microcomputer selects and amplifies information by representing it in a decontextualized manner. The origins of the facts, data, and other representations (the historical and interpretive aspects of knowledge) that appear on the monitor tend to be lost through the amplification-reduction characteristics of the technology. The inability of the technology to represent the tacit dimensions of cultural knowledge, including the metaphorical characteristics of spoken and nonverbal language (which rely heavily upon their relation to contextual use), also remains a problem. Lastly, the way in which the microcomputer amplifies the conceptual and social traits associated with literacy is not fundamentally altered by having the software written in the native language.

Such efforts to adapt instructional software need to be supplemented by an approach to the education of teachers and others connected with educational computer that recognizes the basic difference between computer literacy and computer mechanics, the latter representing the ability to utilize various software programs. As mentioned earlier, literacy involves, in its broadest sense, decoding the language processes that make up a culture. In its deepest sense, it means being able to make explicit the underlying assumptions and conceptual categories encoded in the language processes that are used to sustain a cultural ecology. When literacy is related to educational computing, it should carry this broader and deeper sense of meaning.

Computer literacy, as exercised by the teacher in a Third World country, should involve the ability to make professional judgments about how the technology is influencing the process of cultural transmission. This would require not only an understanding of the teacher's own cultural traditions but also an ability to recognize how borrowed technologies serve as carriers of exogenous cultural values. Computer literacy would thus involve possessing an understanding of culture (including the nature of tradition, and both tacit and analogue forms of knowledge), the metaphorical nature of language (including the native language as well as the cultural orientation embedded in dominant Western languages used for writing instructional software), and the cultural amplification and reduction characteristics of computer technology. In addition, the teacher needs to understand the dynamics of the socialization process in order to recognize when to supplement an instructional program with a historical perspective, how to ground it more in the lifeworld of local custom, and how to demystify it by making explicit the hidden assumptions of the person who wrote the software program. As mentioned earlier, knowing what should be communicated through print and what is more appropriately shared through the spoken word are also critically important professional judgments for teachers to make.

In addition to the policy questions associated with the teacher's relationship to the modernizing process, there is the more obvious and straightforward issue of deciding how to educate Third World teachers to use the microcomputer in educational settings, given the variation in cultural norms in thought and practice. The current approach of sending future educational leaders to a Western country for advanced degrees in educational computing is inadequate (and perhaps even dangerous) if the program of study is narrowly oriented toward learning how to use the technology. In most educational-computing departments, learning how to use a data base, LOGO, or a special instructional program also involves acquiring cultural assumptions about the neutral nature of the computer, the dawning of the Information Age, and the rationalism and individualism associated with being modern. A policy question pertaining to how to educate future educational leaders in the use of microcomputers relates to whether a more prescriptive approach should be taken by Third

World countries in negotiating the development of a special graduate program with specific Western universities that possess genuine strength in the interdisciplinary areas essential for understanding the pedagogical and cultural aspects of educational computing. This would seem an essential improvement over the current situation, in which graduate programs of study are designed by people who are largely blind to the cultural assumptions built into the technology, as well too narrowly specialized to recognize how computing fits into the modernizing process that is now in crisis.

An alternative to sending students to Western countries would be for each country to develop its own interdisciplinary institute for the study of education, technology, and culture, or to develop an institute on a more regional, pancultural basis. Either approach need not exclude Western scholars. More local or regional control over how this important technology is to be integrated into the educational process is vital to insuring that the modernizing process is grounded in a knowledge of the essential categories that the Scollons found in an ancient saying of Confucius:

> The men of old wanting to clarify and diffuse throughout the empire that light which comes from looking straight into the heart and then acting, first set up good government in their own states; wanting good government in their states, they first established order in their own families; wanting order in the home, they first disciplined themselves; desiring self-discipline, they rectified their own hearts; and wanting to rectify their hearts, they sought precise verbal definitions of their inarticulate thoughts; wishing to attain precise verbal definitions, they set out to extend their knowledge to the utmost. This completion of knowledge is rooted in sorting things into organic categories. (Pound, 1969, pp. 29–30)

The understanding of past, place, relationships, and future possibilities, which is essential to people's ability to rebuild culture within themselves, involves an approach to education that does not start with the assumption that language and machines are neutral. Nor is it achieved by the uncritical acceptance of another culture's definition of modernization.

REFERENCES

INDEX

ABOUT THE AUTHOR

References

Adams, Anthony, and Jones, Esmor. 1983. *Teaching Humanities in the Electronic Age*. Milton Keynes, England: Open University Press.

Bateson, Gregory. 1974. *Steps to an Ecology of Mind*. New York: Ballantine.

Becker, Henry Jay. 1983. *Microcomputers in the Classroom: Dreams and Realities*. Eugene, OR: International Council for Computers in Education.

Belenky, Mary Field; Clinchy, Blythe McVicker; Goldberger, Nancy Rule; and Tarule, Jill Mattuck. 1986. *Women's Way of Knowing: The Development of Self, Voice, and Mind*. New York: Basic.

Bellah, Robert N.; Madsen, Richard; Sullivan, William M.; Swidler, Ann; and Tipton, Steven M. 1985. *Habits of the Heart: Individualism and Commitment in American Life*. Berkeley: University of California Press.

Benzon, Bill. 1985. "The Visual Mind and the Macintosh." *Byte* (January): 113–30.

Berger, Peter; Berger, Brigitte; and Kellner, Hansfried. 1974. *The Homeless Mind: Modernization and Consciousness*. New York: Vintage.

Berman, Morris. 1986. "The Cybernetic Dream of the Twenty-First Century." *Journal of Humanistic Psychology* 26 (Spring): 24–51.

Berry, Wendell. 1970. *A Continuous Harmony: Essays Cultural and Agricultural*. New York: Harcourt Brace Jovanovich.

______ . 1986. *The Unsettling of America: Culture and Agriculture*. San Francisco: Sierra Club.

Birnbaum, Joel S. 1985. "Toward the Domestication of Microelectronics." *Computer* (November): 128–40.

Bloom, Alfred. 1981. *The Linguistic Shaping of Thought: A Study in the Impact of Language on Thinking in China and the West*. Hillsdale, NJ: Erlbaum.

Bordo, Susan. 1987. *The Flight to Objectivity: Essays on Cartesianism and Culture*. Albany: State University of New York Press.

Bowers, C. A. 1986. "Nihilism and the State: Implications for an Emancipatory Theory of Education." *Educational Theory* 36 (Summer): 225–33.

______ . 1987a. *Elements of a Post-Liberal Theory of Education*. New York: Teachers College Press.

______ . 1987b. *The Promise of Theory: Education and the Politics of Cultural Change*. New York: Teachers College Press.

______ . 1988. "Teaching a 19th Century Mode of Thinking Through a 20th Century Machine." *Educational Theory*. In press.

Branfman, Fred. 1985. "On the Computer Revolution." *World Policy Journal* 2 (3): 569–86.

Caley, Michael. 1986. "Two Spelling Aids with 'Appleworks'." *The Computing Teacher* 14 (August/September): 38–39.

Callister, Thomas. 1986. *The Effect of Innovative Technical Change on an Elementary School*. Unpublished doctoral dissertation, University of Utah, Salt Lake City.

Carson, Rachel. 1962. *Silent Spring*. Boston: Houghton-Mifflin.

Cazden, Courtney B.; Johns, Vera P.; and Hymes, Dell, eds. 1972. *Functions of Language in the Classroom*. New York: Teachers College Press.

Clayton, Mark. 1987. "A Technology of Big Outlays, Modest Returns." *The Christian Science Monitor* (February 20): 22.

Commoner, Barry. 1972. *The Closing Circle: Nature, Man, and Technology*. New York: Knopf.

"Computer." 1987. *The Register Guard* (Eugene, OR) (February 20): 1 C.

Cooper, Douglas. 1986. "A First Stage Report of an Ethnographic Study of the Apple Classroom of Tomorrow." Eugene, OR.

Cowen, Robert C. 1986. "Genetic Engineering." *The Christian Science Monitor* (September 26): 18–19.

Dasmann, Raymond. 1968. *Environmental Conservation*. 2nd ed. New York: Wiley. (Original work published 1959)

Douglas, Mary. 1975. *Implicit Meanings: Essays in Anthropology*. London: Routledge & Kegan Paul.

Dupuy, Jean-Pierre. 1980. "Myths of the Information Society." In *The Myths of Information: Technology and Postindustrial Culture*, edited by Kathleen Woodward, pp. 3–17. Bloomington: Indiana University Press.

The Eclectic Elementary Geography. 1896. New York: American Book Company.

Educational Technology Center. 1986. *Immigrant: The Irish Experience in Boston, 1840–1870*. Cambridge, MA: Harvard University.

Eliot, T. S. 1943. *Four Quartets*. New York: Harcourt Brace.

Ellul, Jacques. 1964. *The Technological Society*. New York: Vantage. (Original work published 1954)

Faber, Roger J. 1986. *Clockwork Garden: On the Mechanistic Reduction of Living Things*. Amherst: University of Massachusetts Press.

Fischler, Martin A., and Firschein, Oscar. 1986. "Intelligence and the Computer: The Central Role of Representation." *AI Expert* 1 (December): 44.

Foucault, Michel. 1979. *Discipline and Punish: The Birth of the Prison*. New York: Vintage.

______ . 1983. "The Subject and Power." In *Michel Foucault: Beyond Structuralism and Hermeneutics*, edited by Hubert L. Dreyfus and Paul Rabinow, pp. 208–26. Chicago: The University of Chicago Press.

Geertz, Clifford. 1973. *The Interpretation of Cultures*. New York: Basic.

Giddens, Anthony. 1981. *A Contemporary Critique of Historical Materialism*. Berkeley: University of California Press.

Gilligan, Carol. 1982. *In a Different Voice: Psychological Theory and Women's Development*. Cambridge, MA: Harvard University Press.

Goffman, Erving. 1974. *Frame Analysis: An Essay on the Organization of Experience*. New York: Harper.

Goodenough, Ward H. 1981. *Culture, Language, and Society*. Menlo Park, CA: Benjamin/Cummings.

Goody, Jack, ed. 1962. *Literacy in Traditional Societies*.

______ . 1977. *The Domestication of the Savage Mind*. Cambridge: Cambridge University Press.

Gouldner, Alvin W. 1979. *The Future of Intellectuals and the Rise of the New Class*. New York: Seabury Press.

Habermas, Jürgen. 1971. *Toward a Rational Society*. Boston: Beacon Press.

Hall, Edward T. 1977. *Beyond Culture*. Garden City, NJ: Anchor.

Havelock, Eric A. 1963. *Preface to Plato*. Cambridge, MA: Harvard University Press, Belknap Press.

______ . 1986. *The Muse Learns to Write: Reflections on Orality and Literacy from Antiquity to the Present*. New Haven, CT: Yale University Press.

Heidegger, Martin. 1977. *The Question Concerning Technology and Other Essays*, translated by William Lovitt. New York: Harper & Row. (Original work published 1954)

______ . 1982. *On the Way to Language*. New York: Harper & Row.

Horton, Robin. 1982. "Tradition and Modernity Revisited." In *Rationality and Relativism*, edited by Martin Hollis and Steven Lukes, pp. 201–60. Cambridge, MA: MIT Press.

Ihde, Don. 1979. *Technics and Praxis*. Dordrecht, Holland: D. Reidel.

Illich, Ivan. 1977. *Toward a History of Needs*. New York: Pantheon.

Keller, Evelyn Fox. 1985. *Reflections on Gender and Science*. New Haven, CT: Yale University Press.

Kikuchi, Makoto. 1981. "Creativity and Ways of Thinking: The Japanese Style." *Physics Today* (September): 42–45.

Kinzer, Charles K.; Sherwood, Robert D.; and Bransford, John D., eds. 1986. *Computer Strategies for Education: Foundations and Content-Area Applications*. Columbus, OH: Merrill.

Koepp, Stephen. 1986. "The Boss That Never Blinks." *Time* (July 28): 46–47.

Lakoff, Robin. 1975. *Language and Women's Place*. New York: Harper & Row.

Lakoff, George, and Johnson, Mark. 1980. *Metaphors We Live By*. Chicago: University of Chicago Press.

Long, Marion. 1985. "Turncoat of the Computer Revolution." *New Age Journal* (December): 46–54.

Lyotard, Jean-François. 1984. *The Postmodern Condition: A Report on Knowledge*. Minneapolis: University of Minnesota Press.

MacIntyre, Alasdair. 1984. *After Virtue*. 2nd ed. Notre Dame, IN: University of Notre Dame.

McClintock, Robert. 1988. "Marking the Second Frontier." *Teachers College Record* 89 (Spring): 345–51.

McCorduck, Pamela. 1979. *Machines Who Think*. New York: Freeman.

______ . 1985. *The Universal Machine: Confessions of a Technological Optimist*. New York: McGraw-Hill.

McLuhan, T. C. 1971. *Touch the Earth*. New York: Simon & Schuster.

Marx, Gary T., and Sherizen, Sanford. 1986. "Monitoring on the Job." *Technology Review* (November–December): 63–72.

Max Think, Inc. 1986. *Thinking*. Piedmont, CA: Author.

Mazrui, Ali A. 1978. *Political Values and the Educated Class in Africa*. Berkeley: University of California Press.

Minnesota Educational Computing Consortium. 1983. *Oh, Deer!* St. Paul, MN: Author.

______ . 1985. *Oregon Trail*. St. Paul, MN: Author.

Mowshowitz, Abbe. 1984. "Computers and the Myth of Neutrality." *ACM SIGCSE Bulletin* 16 (February): 1–8.

Mueller, Claus. 1973. *The Politics of Communication*. London: Oxford University Press.

Mumford, Lewis. 1934. *Technics and Civilization*. New York: Harcourt, Brace & World.

Naisbitt, John. 1982. *Megatrends: Ten New Directions Transforming Our Lives*. New York: Warner.

Nichol, Jon, and Dean, Jacqueline. 1984. "Pupils, Computers and History Teaching." In *New Horizons in Educational Computing*, edited by Masoud Yazdani, pp. 190–204. Chichester, England: Ellis Horwood.

Nietzsche, Friedrich. 1968. *The Will to Power*. New York: Vintage. (Original work published 1888)

Noble, David F. 1984. *Forces of Production: A Social History of Industrial Automation*. New York: Knopf.

"Numbers Crunch In." 1987. *The Oregonian* (Portland) (February 26): E1.

Oakeshott, Michael. 1962. *Rationalism in Politics*. New York: Basic.

Ong, Walter J. 1977. *Interfaces of the Word: Studies in the Evolution of Consciousness and Culture*. Ithaca, NY: Cornell University Press.

______ . 1982. *Orality and Literacy: The Technologizing of the Word*. London: Methuen.

Ozick, Cynthia. 1986. "The Moral Necessity of Metaphor." *Harper's Magazine* 272 (May): 62–69.

Papert, Seymour. 1980. *Mind Storms: Children, Computers and Powerful Ideas*. New York: Basic.

Pitkin, Hannah F. 1973. *Wittgenstein and Justice*. Berkeley: University of California Press.

Porritt, Jonathan. 1984. *Seeing Green: The Politics of Ecology Explained*. Oxford: Blackwell.

Pound, Ezra. 1969. *Confucius*. New York: New Direction Books.

Ramsey, Sheila. 1984. "Double Vision: Nonverbal Behavior East and West." In

Nonverbal Behavior: Perspectives, Applications, Intercultural Insights, edited by Aaron Wolfgang, pp. 139–67. Toronto: C. J. Hogrefe.

Reddy, Michael J. 1979. "The Conduit Metaphor—A Case of Frame Conflict in Our Language About Language." In *Metaphor and Thought,* edited by Andrew Ortony, pp. 284–324. Cambridge: Cambridge University Press.

Reinhold, Fran. 1986. "An Interview with Seymour Papert." *Electronic Learning* (April): 33–36.

Rhiannon Software. 1984. *Jenny of the Prairie*. Reading, MA: Addison-Wesley.

Rorty, Richard. 1979. *Philosophy and the Mirror of Nature*. Princeton, NJ: Princeton University Press.

Roszak, Theodore. 1986. *The Cult of Information: The Folklore of Computers and the True Art of Thinking*. New York: Pantheon.

Sale, Kirkpatrick. 1986. "Dwellers in the Land: The Bioregional Vision." *Utne Reader* (February/March): 22–34.

Schon, Donald A. 1979. "Generative Metaphor: A Perspective on Problem-Setting in Social Policy." In *Metaphor and Thought,* edited by Andrew Ortony, pp. 254–83. Cambridge: Cambridge University Press.

Schumacher, E. F. 1973. *Small Is Beautiful*. New York: Harper & Row.

Scollon, Ron. 1985. "The Machine Stops: Silence in the Metaphor of Malfunction." In *Perspectives on Silence,* edited by Deborah Tannen and Muriel Saville-Troike, pp. 93–111. Norwood, NJ: Ablex.

Scollon, Ron, and Scollon, Suzanne. 1985. *The Problem of Power*. Haines, AK: Gutenberg Dump.

"A Secular Humanist Declaration." 1981. *New Humanist* 96 (January): 57–60.

Scribner, Sylvia, and Cole, Michael. 1981. *The Psychology of Literacy*. Cambridge, MA: Harvard University Press.

Shils, Edward. 1981. *Tradition*. Chicago: University of Chicago Press.

Siegel, Lenny, and Markoff, John. 1985. *The High Cost of High Tech: The Dark Side of the Chip*. New York: Harper & Row.

Siegel, Martin A., and Davis, Dennis M. 1986. *Understanding Computer-Based Education*. New York: Random House.

Simons, Geoff. 1985. *The Biology of Computer Life*. Boston: Birkhauser.

______ . 1986. *Silicon Shock: The Menance of the Computer*. Oxford: Blackwell.

Sloan, Douglas, ed. 1984. *The Computer in Education: A Critical Perspective*. New York: Teachers College Press.

Snyder, Gary. 1977. *The Old Ways*. San Francisco: City Lights.

______ . 1980. "On Earth Geography." In *The Real Work: Interviews and Talks, 1964–1969,* pp. 70–78. New York: New Directions.

Snyder, Tom. 1985a. *The Other Side*. Cambridge, MA: Tom Snyder Productions.

______ . 1985b. *Resource Guide: The Other Side*. Cambridge, MA: Tom Snyder Productions.

______ . (no date). *Integrating Computers into the Social Studies Classroom: Questions and Answers*. Draft paper. Cambridge, MA: Snyder Productions.

Snyder, Tom, and Palmer, Jane. 1986. *In Search of the Most Amazing Thing: Children, Education and Computers*. Reading, MA: Addison-Wesley.

Spender, Dale. 1984. "Defining Reality: A Powerful Tool." In *Language and Power*, edited by Cheris Kramarae, Muriel Schulz, and William M. O'Barr, pp. 193–201. Beverly Hills, CA: Sage Publications.

Tannen, Deborah. 1986. *That's Not What I Meant!* New York: William.

Tannen, Deborah, and Saville-Troike, Muriel, eds. 1985. *Perspectives on Silence*. Norwood, NJ: Ablex.

Taylor, Robert, ed. 1980. *The Computer in the Schools: Tutor, Tools, Tutee*. New York: Teachers College Press.

Turkle, Sherry. 1984. *The Second Self: Computers and the Human Spirit*. New York: Simon & Schuster.

Turing, A. M. 1936. "On Computable Numbers, with an Application to the Entscheidungsproblem." In *Proceedings of the London Mathematics Society*. 2d ser., 42:230–65. London: C. F. Hodgson.

Van Deusen, Robert M., and Donham, Jean. 1986–87. "The Teacher's Role in Using the Computer to Teach Thinking Skills." *The Computing Teacher* 14 (December/January): 32–34.

Wedman, John F. 1986. "Making Software More Useful." *The Computing Teacher* (November): 11–14.

Weizenbaum, Joseph. 1976. *Computer Power and Human Reason: From Judgment to Calculation*. New York: Freeman.

Wheeler, Fay. 1987. "The New Ready-Made Databases: What They Offer Your Classroom." *Classroom Computer Learning* 7 (March): 28–32.

Whorf, Benjamin Lee. 1968. "Science and Linguistics." In *Everyman His Way*, edited by Alan Dundes, pp. 318–29. Berkeley: University of California Press.

Winograd, Terry, and Flores, Fernando. 1986. *Understanding Computers and Cognition*. Norwood, NJ: Ablex.

Wresch, William. 1985. *A Practical Guide to Computer Uses in the English/Language Arts Classroom*. Englewood Cliffs, NJ: Prentice-Hall.

Index

About the Author

C. A. BOWERS teaches Education and Social Thought in the College of Education at the University of Oregon. His previous publications include *The Progressive Educator and the Depression: The Radical Years* (1969), *Cultural Literacy for Freedom* (1974), *The Promise of Theory: Education and the Politics of Cultural Change* (1984), and *Elements of a Post-Liberal Theory of Education* (1987).